Copyright and Trade

Notice

IMPORTANT NOTE TO OUR READERS

Disney's
CALIFORNIA ADVENTURE
DETECTIVE

An INDEPENDENT Guide
to Exploring the Trivia, Secrets
and Magic of the Park
Dedicated to California

Kendra Trahan

By Kendra Trahan
with
Portrait Illustrations by Brian McKim
Illustrations by Karl Yamauchi
Photography by Debbie Smith

Disney's California Adventure Detective by Kendra Trahan

Published by
PermaGrin Publishing, Inc.
27758 Santa Margarita Parkway #379
Mission Viejo, CA 92691
www.themeparkdetective.com

Publisher's cataloging in Publication Data
Library of Congress Control: 2008932517
Trahan, Kendra D.
    Disney's California Adventure Detective/ by Kendra Trahan
    p.cm
    includes bibliography and index.

Disneyland Resort (Calif.) —History 2. Amusement Parks (Calif.) I. Trahan, Kendra D. 1967- II. Title

ISBN 978-0-9717464-5-9

Printed in the United States of America
15 14 13 12 11 10 9 8 7 6 5 4 3 2 1

ACKNOWLEDGMENTS

Disney's California Adventure Park has had just a few years of history, which made it especially exciting because this Park was built and opened locally and in my lifetime. Being able to share the experience and learn from the many others who were there opening day is a major event.

Strong contributors who reviewed content are: Chris and Summer Contes, Dave Smith, Heather Dagle, David Doug Marsh, Benji Breithart, Daniel Kaplan, Debbie Smith, Rolly Crump, Harrison Price, David Laurendeau, Lindsey Jackson, Philo Barnhart, Dennis Tanida, Scott McTeir, Gary Schaengold, Patty Humphrey & sons Taylor, Channing, Garrett and Lewis. More contributors include: Donna Pendleton, Darrel Lansing, Jimmy Moreno Jr., John Turner, Angela Bean, Suzanne Bennett, Mary Parker, Paul Schnebelen, Linda & Scott Barton, Gregory Blum, Alan Nicholson and Dan Demeyere.

I wish to make a special thank you to my editors Tom and Sara Graves who separately and tirelessly checked and rechecked for typos and grammatical errors. Again, a thank you to Bob Swingle at Lightbourne Inc., who shares two alma maters and two books with me. I'd recommend him in a heartbeat. Again he designed the interior and a cover that encourages most shoppers to buy.

Another thank-you to photographer Debbie Smith who captured photos of Disney's California Adventure even before I knew I would write a book about it, but also before it was even finished. Together we covered this Park thoroughly and know just about every inch.

Thank you to my good friend Karl Yamauchi who has more talent than is realized. I hope your wish of working for Disney as an artist comes true. Keep wishing on that star!

Brian McKim, you're the easiest guy to work with and your portraits are great. I'm proud to work with you again.

To the Disney Imagineers, cast members and family members who graciously shared their stories, time and support thank you. Disney's California Adventure is phenomenal, so let's help others appreciate it.

It's essential to thank Terri Hardin for your encouragement and faith.

To my husband, Russell, who gave me the courage and support to keep going. He's one of the biggest enablers of them all, and I love him for it!

This book is dedicated
to my dear friends in California.
Specifically Heather, Jamon, Alex,
Shannon, Robert, Chris, and Summer.
You make the Golden State, well, Golden!

Contents

Photo by Debbie Smith

Sun Wheel overlooking Paradise Bay.

Introduction

The purpose of this book is to uncover the trivia, tributes and details that the Imagineers created in Disney's California Adventure Park. According to Dave Smith (head of Disney Archives, author and columnist), this is the first book to do so, and hopefully won't be the last. At a first glance, Disney's California Adventure seems to be an average theme park, but sitting next to Disneyland, it is hard to compete. Disneyland has three times the attractions and a 46-year head start. Disney's California Adventure had some really big shoes to fill. After a while, once you visit Disney's California Adventure a few times, it does create its own magic. The details are there for you to uncover if you look.

Let's start with some of the common Disney terminology to reduce confusion later on.

Disney, as with any other corporation in America, loves its acronyms and creates its own vocabulary. So it's appropriate to help you understand some of the lingo and to help you sound like an expert. While the Walt Disney Company executives were hesitant to shorten Disney's California Adventure to DCA, the public and cast members eventually won out on that acronym. With 4 syllables alone in "California," this Park was screaming for an acronym. If you want to sound like a local, it's "the Park," for Disneyland and "DCA" for Disney's California Adventure.

Out of respect, "Disneyland" isn't shortened unless you say "the Park," or "my Park." Actually, locals often call Disneyland "my Park" because Walt Disney gave it to them. In his opening address he says, "To all who come to this happy place, welcome. Disneyland is your land . . ." So it's no wonder the local population is dedicated to preserving its heritage.

Next is the term "cast member," which is the word used to refer to an employee. This dates back to Walt Disney wanting to cast people for roles in his Park, like you would cast people for roles in a movie. The term "customer" is rarely used, but instead "guest." This idea was created by Walt as you are a "guest" in his Park and he probably hopes you'll behave like one.

The area in the Park where guests walk around is referred to as "on-stage" and cast members are expected to uphold specific behaviors that are clearly defined. This is all part of the show so that guests who traveled all over the country can feel that the Disney Parks are a clean, polite and wholesome place to bring the family. Conversely the "cast members only" area is called "Back Stage," and cast members are allowed to relax a little more there; cell phones can be used, smoking and eating are allowed, costumes can be untucked and so on.

"Imagineer" is the term used to describe the engineers, architects, artists, etc., who designed and built the Park. The term was created by Walt to integrate Imagination and Engineer.

Check out the back of the book. It includes a glossary to help you understand some of the other terms.

How to use this book:

Initially, this book was written with annual pass-holders and cast members in mind. These readers will sit down and read it cover to cover because they know where they're going and will have fun making mental notes of what to check out on their next visits. It's fun to see this group fill the book with post-it notes referencing some small details they missed in previous trips.

If you're a first time visitor to Disney's California Adventure, former advice was to put this book down and go play! But a first-time visitor to Disneyland explained to me that their first visit to Disneyland was enhanced by Disneyland Detective, so with great hope Disney's California Adventure Detective will do the same. There is nothing like experiencing something new for the first time. Relax and enjoy yourself and pick up the small details that are most interesting to you.

If you grew up in California, then many of the state tributes in Disney's California Adventure may seem obvious. If you're a transplant or tourist to California, this book may assist you in understanding some of the lesser-known bits of California history the Imagineers were going for.

Other people may carry the book with them and when there is a lull in the day, pull the book out of the backpack and read about the attraction they are about to see: "What's special about this attraction?" or "what should I look for in here?"

HIDDEN MICKEY

Young people and young-at-heart have caught on to the great scavenger hunt of Hidden Mickeys. The craze started on an Internet site where people would spot Hidden Mickeys and make posts. Hidden Mickeys will be labeled in boxes like this one. So if you want to spend your day going on a Hidden Mickey scavenger hunt, let this book be your guide. To make it easier, the first appendix lists all the Hidden Mickeys in order so that you can check off all that you've found and list any new ones that come up.

For those who aren't aware of what a Hidden Mickey is, it is a symbol, usually three circles forming the shape of the head of Mickey Mouse. The ear circles should be equal size, while the head circle is larger than the ear circles. The most common shape of a Hidden Mickey is shown here, although sometimes you may see a silhouette or a full-body Mickey.

Hidden Mickeys are scattered throughout the Park. Occasionally, Imagineers or Disney cast members may create them for fun. The practice started at EPCOT, and although the Walt Disney Company recognizes Hidden Mickeys, they do not have an official list. Hidden Mickeys may come and go at will, so that is part of the fun, too. All the Hidden Mickeys in this book have been verified by the author and are "on-stage" and won't get you into any trouble. If a Hidden Mickey is a little subjective, you decide if it's a true Hidden Mickey or not.

There are basically three types of Hidden Mickey. The first is the Imagineer-planned ones that are not easily changed aspects of an attraction. The second type is Cast Member Hidden Mickeys, where props can easily be arranged to form the famous silhouette. Thirdly, there are accidental Hidden Mickeys where, through no real planning, nature has created the proper proportions. It's amazing how frequently Hidden Mickeys appear naturally.

TREASURES & TRIVIA

Once in a while there is a special prop worth noticing. There are a few television props or just interesting tidbits of information worth sharing. When you see this symbol, you may want to give it a glance to enhance your experience.

LESSON TO LEARN

Sometimes students, or students of life, need inspiration to read a new book or write a report. Disney's California Adventure is riddled with just that type of inspiration. Lesson to Learn will refer to books about a particular subject worth reading, people or places in history worth researching, etc. This section should be especially useful for teachers and students or anyone who loves to learn.

OPENING DAY ATTRACTION

This is a new addition to the Disneyland Detective series. If you want to see if the attraction was open and running on opening day, in this case February 8, 2001, then look for this logo.

DISNEY MYTH vs. DISNEY URBAN LEGEND

One goal of this book is to distinguish the difference between Disney myth and Disney urban legend. In fact, it's probably best to identify stories that are urban legend so that future generations won't believe that these stories are true. Both instances are creative fiction, but only Disney myths are designed to be there.

The Disney myth is the story created by the Imagineers to set the theme or mood for the attraction. Fast Pass will cut short the queue and sometimes deny the rider to get the full effect of the Disney myth. Other times, the myth may be so subtle that it isn't quite obvious to people while they are enjoying time with their family and friends. Disney's California Adventure Detective will uncover as many of the Disney myths as possible to enhance your experience.

Then there is Disney urban legend. Urban legends are typically made up by guests or cast members and although aren't true, are difficult to disprove. If anything, Disney urban legends provide some interesting stories while waiting in line. This book will use the distinction to separate the two types of stories.

BECOMING A TRUE Disney's California Adventure DETECTIVE

Part of the fun of being a Disney's California Adventure Detective is that you enjoy the subtle changes to the Park. The phrase, "See you at the C" started to catch on and would mean that you'd meet someone at the huge letter C for C-A-L-I-F-O-R-N-I-A that is spelled out at the entrance at the Park. Or you might hear, "Or if you're late, you can go to L."

Unlike Disneyland that was polished by Walt Disney, and is therefore sacred to some guests. DCA is different as the annual pass-holders and cast members eagerly await changes. Watching it grow and evolve has been exciting. Future editions of this book will try to keep up to date on the attractions, Hidden Mickeys and other fun trivia. For regular visitors,

keep notes and share your findings on the website: www.themeparkdetective.com.

At the time of print, Disney's California Adventure is about to receive a significant investment, possibly adding another new land, transportation around the Park and many other enhancements.

Something else that's new is an interactive scavenger game called the *DCA Detective Chase*. For a small fee you may purchase this two-hour foot rally by going to the website at www.themeparkdetective.com. Great for families, parties or organizations who want to share a team-building experience, you'll see Disney's California Adventure like you've never seen it before.

Theme Park Detective

The Story Behind the Book: 'Disneyland Detective'

Tuesday, June 12, 2007

'Disneyland Detective,' Disney Treasures

Disneyland Detective: An Independent Guide to Discovering Disney's Legend, Lore, & Magic This enthusiastic investigation of Disneyland's hidden treasures leads both first-time visitors and aficionados through the legendary theme park while pointing out tiny surprises around each turn. Helpfully organized as a reading tour, this guidebook features the whereabouts of many of Disneyland's secrets, including... »»»

Walt's Barn in Marceline

Walt's Barn Raising Dedication Although Walt Disney was born in Chicago Illinois, he considered his home town Marceline Missouri. When he was a young boy he grew up on a farm in Marceline and the little town made a lasting impression on him. In 2001 in honor of Walt's 100th Birthday, Marceline... »»»

Our Service Theme

We create happiness by providing enchanting information about Disneyland for Disney fans everywhere.

Inside Sections...
Book Reviews
Disney History
Disneyland

Key Information
Buy Now
About Us
Media Resources
Meeting Planners
Contact Us
Terms of Use
Privacy Policy

Search

Photos by Debbie Smith

Upper photo: *Paradise Pier in the background looks about ready. Grizzly River Peak is beginning to take shape and the monorail track remains unchanged in the foreground.*
Lower photo: *Disney's Grand Californian Hotel and Soarin' are under construction simultaneously.*

Chapter 1

HISTORY OF
Disney's California Adventure

With the addition of Disney's California Adventure, the property including Disneyland Park was renamed The Disneyland Resort. The resort encompasses not just Disneyland and Disney's California Adventure, but three hotels; the world's largest parking structure; and Downtown Disney, which offers shopping and dining. When the Mickey & Friends parking structure was built, it was the largest in the continental United States and claims to hold 10,242 vehicles.

LESSON TO LEARN

Buzz Price was named a Disney Legend in 2004 and is highly honored for his contributions to the development of theme parks. To learn more about Buzz and his experiences with Walt, get yourself a copy of his book, *Walt's Revolution! By the Numbers.*

TREASURE & TRIVIA

In 2002, the Detroit Metropolitan Wayne County Airport built a structure with more than 11,000 spaces and stole the title of the world's largest parking structure away from Mickey & Friends. That's okay, the next world's largest parking structure is at Tokyo Disneyland.

In 1953, and fresh out of Stanford Business School, Harrison "Buzz" Price was hired by Walt Disney to determine where the best place to build Disneyland would be. Buzz directed Walt to an orange grove in Anaheim, Calif., because it was toward the center of where the Los Angeles population was growing, but also because Interstate 5 would lead people there. Walt purchased 160 acres, used the first 60 acres to build Disneyland, but left the other 100 acres for parking. It took the next 40 years for Disney's California Adventure to develop on paper, but according to Buzz,

Walt had plans to build "a second gate" very early on.

Many years later, the idea of a second Park in Anaheim was discussed. Michael Eisner understood that guests spent two weeks at Walt Disney World, but usually only one day at Disneyland. In 1989, he asked a few Imagineers to develop a plan for a second gate. Ideas about "WestCOT" were discussed, resulting in a second gate that would be similar to EPCOT at Walt Disney World in Orlando, Fla. The plans for expansion were very detailed and Disney made public announcements in May of 1991. The plans included new hotels and an expansion of Disneyland.

WestCOT was intended to be an upgrade of EPCOT. Initial plans set out that guests could stay in the World Showcase areas overnight, with a super-ride connecting the countries. This 45-minute water ride had five stops with nine-minute shows in between. Ride vehicles would be a lot like the Jungle Cruise, and the attraction tour would introduce you to one of the Four Corners of the World: Europe, Asia, Africa, and the Middle East. This long ride would take people from land to land and discuss their cultures and history. Guests could step out and enjoy a little of what these cultures had to offer. Due to a combination of cost and local opposition, the plans were dropped July 17, 1995. Many locals were not very excited about a

300' gold sphere that would dominate the skyline. The sphere took on some modifications of size and shape, but eventually the whole concept was cancelled.

TREASURE & TRIVIA

EPCOT stands for Experimental Prototype Community of Tomorrow. Today, cast members have a lot of other meanings for EPCOT such as: Employee Paychecks Come Out Thursday or Excruciating Polyester Costumes of Torture. Guests declare that EPCOT stands for Every Person Comes Out Tired.

For a while, ocean-type concepts for a second gate in Long Beach were created and later used at Tokyo DisneySea, however it was Michael Eisner who put the resources behind the Imagineers to create an original idea.

In early August 1995, Eisner called a meeting of about 36 Disney executives from Walt Disney Imagineering (WDI) to Colorado. The team was asked to attend a three-day creative session to develop initial plans for a long-awaited second theme park next to Disneyland. The meeting came to be known as the "Aspen charette." The term "charette" means "cram session" for Disney people, dating back to when Walt Disney would use the term for storyboard conferences.

It is reported that Imagineer Barry Braverman mentioned to his wife before he left for the meeting, "Maybe we could do a Park about California."

Once the meeting was underway and introductions between Walt Disney Attractions and Imagineering had taken place, the meeting broke into four groups. Barry pitched the idea to his team, but they were more excited about developing some other concepts.

In another part of the meeting, Marty Sklar, vice president of Imagineering, suggested a Park about California. His group supported it and pitched it to Michael Eisner.

Eisner wrote on a small card "Disney's California, the beach, Hollywood, the workplace" after hearing the pitch about Parks, aquariums, oceans and Route 66. This small card from the Aspen charette and a short pitch about California would develop into Disney's California Adventure.

After many months and many follow-up meetings, the California Adventure project was given a green light and Barry Braverman was named the executive producer. Barry was a 20-year Disney veteran who had been working at EPCOT for five years. In Florida, he was in charge of the design and renovation of *The Land, Innoventions* and *The Universe of Energy.*

On July 17, 1996, Paul Pressler, chairman of Walt Disney Parks and Resorts, made an official announcement that Disneyland

Photos by Debbie Smith

would see a $1.4 billion expansion.

The Imagineers had budgeted 55 acres of the Disneyland parking lot to build Disney's California Adventure. The parking lot was surrounded by hotels, restaurants, neighborhoods and Disneyland. No green fields or trees, just wide open spaces for construction traffic. The land was flat, but eventually a mountain and a lake would be constructed. The challenge was to make Grizzly Peak and Paradise Bay look as if they were natural and had been there all along.

Walt Disney had commented that he was always disappointed that he couldn't afford more land in Southern California and that the neighborhood around Harbor Boulevard had become a chaotic series of crowded hotels. Barry Braverman was given a chance to fix some of that. In partnering with Anaheim city officials, Braverman was permitted to redesign not just a new theme park, but the entire resort area, a new hotel, the parking structure, Downtown Disney and 22 intersections around the resort. In addition to these on-property changes, a new name and a new logo were in order. It was named "The Disneyland Resort." All the off-property redesign is referred to as the "Anaheim Resort" by the city of Anaheim.

On October 14, 1998, a preview center was opened near Disneyland to show guests what they could expect from Disney's California Adventure.

TREASURE & TRIVIA

Disneyland and Disney's California Adventure have a lot in common. When Disneyland opened July 17, 1955, it was only 60 acres with about 20 attractions. Disney's California Adventure would open with 55 acres and 22 attractions.

Alan Rose, vice president of Project Management, focused on the organization of the construction. He studied reports on traffic analysis of 22 key intersections to prevent gridlock during construction. One issue was parking for 3,000 workers, 15 general contractors, 500 subcontractors and many of the 1,900 Imagineers. Instead of parking personal vehicles next to the location, like most construction jobs, thousands of parking lots were leased, and buses shuttled people to and from the site. Delivery trucks created another issue and eventually a special delivery area was created where arrivals would stand by via radio and receive notification when it was ok to go into the construction area.

Alan Rose was quoted in the Spring 2001 *Disney Magazine* as saying, "Getting material in, getting people in, getting people out, a crane coming in at noon, material leaving at two o'clock—it would be gridlock out there unless we really worked with all of our teams and

contractors to develop a program that allowed people to move and work to go on." Walter Wrobleski, vice president of Construction Management, admitted, "It had to work like a Swiss watch."

Another unusual challenge was building the hotel around the monorail track. The hotel design had to compensate for the transportation system, while appearing natural. The solution was an open-air courtyard surrounded by sequoia trees. The monorail glides over the

courtyard and quietly through the hotel.

Five-and-a-half years after the initial announcement, 18 months of construction and $1.4 billion later, Disney's California Adventure opened on time and on budget. Disney's California Adventure represents the different topographies, cultures and history of California, and brings to life why people travel to California. The Northern Sierra is represented by the Grizzly Peak Recreation area, Napa Valley and many of the wineries are illustrated in the Golden Vine Winery. The Pacific Wharf area is reminiscent of the San Francisco Bay Area, and the glamour of Hollywood is in the forefront.

California state history is sprinkled all over the Park. For example, the California poppy, which is the state flower, fills the mural and entrance stores. In fact, there is a lot of orange in the resort. Maybe the reason is because it is in Orange County, or maybe because the site was formerly an orange grove.

JANUARY 7, 2001

(one month prior to the grand opening)

On January 7, 2001, DCA had a soft opening for Disney cast members only. Six preview days offered the chance for cast members or special guests to get a sneak look at Disney's California Adventure. More than 60,000 tickets were distributed, and although the rains were heavy, many people came to see the offerings of Disney's California Adventure. This gave the new Disney's California Adventure cast members a chance to learn how to operate the ride systems with people around. Fundraisers for a Children's Hospital and other charities made the Park accessible for certain locals.

JANUARY 11, 2001

Downtown Disney district hosted its press opening on January 11. This public area (not requiring an admission ticket) offers 300,000 square feet of shopping, dining and entertainment. Familiar sites such as ESPN Zone, Rainforest Caf?, House of Blues, Ralph Brennan's Jazz Kitchen, AMC Theater and the world's second largest World of Disney Store anchor Downtown Disney.

TREASURE & TRIVIA

If Downtown Disney has the second largest World of Disney Store, where is the largest? The largest is Downtown Disney Marketplace at Walt Disney World in Florida.

FEBRUARY 6, 2001

February 6, the Grand Californian Hotel & Spa was dedicated by Tony Bruno, the general manager of the hotel. Featuring 751 guest rooms and a six-floor atrium lobby of 8,000 square feet, the Grand Californian is the new flagship of the Disneyland Resort. It's the first hotel in California to be built by Disney and inside of a theme park, yet it is a peaceful and private retreat. The state's first lady, Sharon Davis, was on hand to help dedicate the building. One of the highlights of the dedication was the parade of hotel cast members as they filled the stage, walls and balconies of the hotel, waving banners and welcoming guests. The hotel is modeled after the Arts and Crafts Movement, which was popular in California in the early 1900s. It's the first commercial building in this style, and a true work of art. You can read more about the hotel in chapter 8.

Later that same day, the corporate sponsors each had a dedication ceremony and were given a beautiful, inscribed crystal plate with the

DCA logo. The opening day sponsors were primarily California-based companies, such as Karl Strauss Brewery, Boudin Bakery, Robert Mondavi and Mission Tortilla Factory. Corporate giants Caterpillar and McDonald's both got their start in California and are early sponsors of DCA.

TREASURE & TRIVIA

The McDonald brothers, Richard and Maurice, got their start at a hot-dog stand called the Airdrome in Arcadia, Calif., in 1937. They moved to San Bernardino in 1940 and began operating McDonald's. The original restaurant is gone, but the base of the original sign on the original site is marked by a plaque. Arcadia is about 35 miles from Disneyland Resort. San Bernardino is about 50 miles northeast of Disney.

The night before the grand opening, Disney's California Adventure rolled out the red carpet for celebrities. The celebrity premiere rocked with performances by the Beach Boys, accompanied by John Stamos on drums and guitar. Guests included Roy E. Disney, Drew Carey, Dick Van Dyke, Mickey Rooney, Jack Nicholson, Frankie Muniz, Melissa Joan Hart, David Hasselhoff, Laurie Metcalf, Art Linkletter, Buddy Ebsen, Tracey Ullman, Haley Joel Osment, Dennis Franz, Rick Schroder, Tim Allen, George Lucas, the Goo Goo Dolls, Jodi Benson, Colin Mochrie, Sela Ward, Michael Boatman and Whoopi Goldberg.

FEBRUARY 7, 2001

On February 7, some key attractions were dedicated. Paul Pressler was again on hand to dedicate "Soarin' Over California" with Jeana Yeager and Dick Rutan, pilots of the Voyager. ABC daytime drama queen Linda Dano hosted the dedication of the Soap Opera Bistro, a short-lived restaurant built like the television sets of some of the most popular ABC Soaps. Kermit the Frog and Charlie Rivkin, the president and CEO of Jim Henson Company joined Cynthia Harriss, Disneyland Resort president, to dedicate Muppet Vision 3D. Lastly, Bob Iger, president and chief operating officer of the Walt Disney Company, dedicated the Golden Dreams attraction with Whoopi Goldberg. Whoopi was given a 3D representation of the statues inside the theater, modeled after her.

Meanwhile, hundreds of fans camped overnight on the streets of Disneyland so that they could be the first to enter Disney's California Adventure. People began to line up around 5 a.m. on February 7, a whole day early, to be the first official guests and to watch the opening day celebration of Disney's California Adventure Park. In the early morning hours, the line was moved from the parking lot to inside Disneyland, where guests lined up along Main Street U.S.A. down Matterhorn Way. Many people spent the night on the asphalt of Disneyland. A steady stream of guests flowed in as Thursday morning approached. The line veered around the tea cups and through Fantasyland.

OPENING DAY: FEBRUARY 8, 2001

On February 8, 2001, at 7:45 a.m. at the Main Entry Plaza, the opening ceremony began. With Olympic style flair and a few Vegas-style costumes, the Park was dedicated. Roy E. Disney was the first to greet the audience, followed by Michael Eisner and Mickey Mouse. Michael Eisner read the dedication, which is bronzed in front of the Sunshine Plaza. Several guests who were present at the opening of Disneyland were introduced, including Art Linkletter, Buddy Ebsen and three of the original Mouseketeers; Bobby Burgess, Tommy Cole and Sharon Baird.

The crowd then was introduced to the first guests to enter DCA, the Klepper family from Murrieta, Calif. The family was selected February 1, as Nicci the daughter, had been a Special Olympics athlete since 1989. Also invited to kick off the opening ceremony were Michael Schwartner and Christine Graves, who were the first children to enter

the gates of Disneyland July 18, 1955. There is a famous photograph of Walt Disney with Michael and Christine taken on that special day, and it seemed fitting that they be present for California's second gate.

With great fanfare, fireworks and dramatic music, Disney's California Adventure Park opened February 8, 2001, at 8 a.m.

The opening dedication read by Michael Eisner was modeled after that of Disneyland and the Magic Kingdom. It reads:

"To all who believe in the power of dreams . . . Welcome! Disney's California Adventure opens its golden gates to you. Here we pay tribute to the dreamers of the past . . . the native people, explorers, immigrants, aviators, entrepreneurs and entertainers who built the Golden State. And we salute a new generation of dreamers who are creating the wonders of tomorrow . . . from the silver screen to the computer screen . . . from the fertile farmlands to the far reaches of space. Disney's California Adventure celebrates the richness and diversity of California . . . its land, its people, its spirit and above all, the dreams that it continues to inspire."

LESSON TO LEARN

The dedication was given by Michael Eisner who, at that time, was the chairman and CEO of the Walt Disney Company. In 2004, he was asked by the stockholders to release one of these positions. After the highly publicized stockholder meeting, he resigned as CEO of the Walt Disney Company. A few months later he announced his retirement (resignation) at the end of his contract in September 2005. He served 22 years as leader of the Walt Disney Company. To learn more about his career, read his autobiography *Work in Progress*. Bob Iger assumed his role as president.

Here is a list of the opening day attractions:

Jim Henson's Muppet Vision 3D
Superstar Limo
Hyperion Theater
Disney Animation
Soarin' Over California
Grizzly River Run
Redwood Creek Challenge Trail
Golden Dreams
Golden Vine Winery
Seasons of the Vine
It's Tough to be a Bug!
Mission Tortilla Factory
The Boudin Bakery
King Triton's Carousel
California Screamin'
Sun Wheel
Maliboomer
Midway Games
Orange Stinger
Mulholland Madness
S.S. rustworthy
Jumpin' Jellyfish
Golden Zephyr

For collectors, Disney's California Adventure inspired a lot of premiums to collect. *The Disneyland Resort Line*, the company issued newsletter, was printed in color on opening day. The back cover published the 20,000 cast member names. Cast members were also given digital watches that ran backwards to count down to the grand opening. Opening day maps were distributed to all the guests who entered Disney's California Adventure.

Photo by Kendra Trahan

For the frequent traveler to Walt Disney World in Florida, Disney's California Adventure will seem to be a combination of many of the attractions from MGM Studios and Animal Kingdom. Some carnival games were added along with some shining moments of new "E-Ticket" attractions in each land.

Oddly, Disney's California Adventure had the title of Disney's newest Park for only seven months. While California was getting its new addition, Tokyo DisneySea was being built simultaneously. Tokyo DisneySea boasted a budget almost twice that of DCA and many state-of-the-art attractions. After waiting 45 years for a second Park, some guests felt a little resentful. Many of the attractions at DCA were recycled from Florida, with only a few exceptions. Soarin', Screamin' and the Animation Building would become the shining stars of Disney's California Adventure.

The months following the opening of Disney's California Adventure were somewhat slow. Orange County suffered from one of the coldest winters and springs in years. Also, Disney's California Adventure, with only 22 attractions next to Disneyland with its 60 attractions, was offered at the same price, which put off some potential visitors. It would take time for the Park to allow park hopper passes and annual passes into both Parks. Yet people would continue to flow into Disneyland, which started to enjoy one of its best years in attendance. Disneyland has its attendance base well established, but Disney's California Adventure would have to fight with other attractions in Southern California such as Knott's Berry Farm, SeaWorld, San Diego Zoo, Universal Studios, Six Flags Magic Mountain, Hollywood and the Southern California beaches.

Then, just seven months after the opening of Disney's California Adventure, the terrorist attacks of September 11, 2001 hit and the economy and tourism dropped significantly. Both Disneyland and Disney's California Adventure did not open that day as news of the events happened early enough in the morning that the West Coast had time to respond. In the months following 9/11 Walt Disney World in Florida suffered the most because the Orlando tourism industry relies on people flying into the city, while Disneyland and Disney's California Adventure rely on tourism primarily from the greater Los Angeles area. Ultimately, although attendance dropped, the Disneyland Resort was not affected as much. In its opening year, Disney's California Adventure didn't reach its projected attendance goals, but the next few years it saw significant improvements, both in attendance and in attractions.

Park hopper passes and annual passes now allow guests to flow between Disneyland and Disney's

California Adventure. For the thrill seekers, another "E-Ticket" attraction, Twilight Zone Tower of Terror, was added. For the little tykes, a new land was added, "a bug's land." As for the general public, Disney's California Adventure is carving a niche for itself, as it hosts many special events such as The X-Games, Rockin' at the Bay, ABC Soap Opera Weekend and ABC Prime Time Preview Weekend events. California fans were thrilled when their much-loved *Main Street Electrical Parade* found a new name and a new home as *Disney's Electrical Parade* in DCA.

Imagineers aggressively continue to add new attractions and new lands to Disney's California Adventure. Some attractions, such as *Superstar Limo* and *Who Wants to Be a Millionaire?* have been phased out. Restaurants such as ABC Soap Opera Bistro, Wolfgang Puck's Avalon Cove and the Lucky Fortune Cookery have closed or been altered. The shows and parades have also had turnover, including *Eureka, Luminaria* and *Steps in Time.* As the Park evolves, it will be exciting to see how Disney's California Adventure finds its niche.

Photo by Debbie Smith

One of the original F7 diesel California Zephyr locomotives that brought people from Chicago to Los Angeles.

Chapter 2

Promenade & Sunshine Plaza

The promenade, or entrance, to Disney's California Adventure is unique in a couple of different ways. While it directly faces Disneyland, no other theme park sits face to face with another. The promenade is made up of thousands of personalized bricks that guests and cast members purchased. (You may request brochures for ordering a brick at the Disneyland City Hall or DCA Guest Relations.)

Once you look directly at the entrance of Disney's California Adventure from the promenade, it is designed to look like a postcard. At the bottom of the giant 3D postcard are sculptural letters that spell C-A-L-I-F-O-R-N-I-A. The letters stand 11 1/2-feet tall. The monorail track is disguised as the Golden Gate Bridge with a sun sculpture sitting at the top. Together with the backdrop of the murals, the entrance plaza is a favorite place to take pictures.

Photo by Debbie Smith

TREASURE & TRIVIA

Notice the glass pieces in the pavement behind each of the letters. If you go to the giant "L" and walk toward the turnstiles, keep a sharp eye on the ground at the glass pieces. You may spot some glass pieces that spell the name "Ana" in the pavement. "Ana" is next to a seam with a section of beige concrete. Ana could be for Anaheim, or it could be an Imagineer or artist or the family member of an Imagineer. So far, no one has come forward to claim the reference.

HIDDEN MICKEY

There is a Hidden Mickey in the glass pieces on the ground. Go to the letter "R" and look toward turnstile number 8. Follow the concrete sections on the ground; the Hidden Mickey is past the second section to the left of the seam and about one foot away from where the red concrete ends. The Hidden Mickey is made of glass and is about three inches wide. Although the glass piece may be cracked, the shape clearly is an intended Hidden Mickey.

Flanking the sides of the postcard are 10,600-square-foot landscape murals. The murals were conceived and painted by Imagineering VP and Executive Designer Tim Delaney. The mosaic murals are shaped like mountains with California icons sprinkled throughout. Spanning 210 feet long, the murals are made of 12,000 pieces of hand-cast ceramic tiles made by Theodora Kurkchiev. Although Disney artists rarely get the chance to sign their work, Theodora Kurkchiev and Tim Delaney were allowed to. You can find the autographs tucked behind the first entrance to the Greetings from California gift shop on the left.

As you enter Disney's California Adventure, the mural on the left has many recognizable landmarks. See if you can identify:

- Yosemite Half Dome and El Capitan Mountain
- A drive-through giant sequoia tree
- Mt. Shasta
- Stripes of cropfields
- California sea lions and California pelicans
- Catalina Casino (See Lesson to Learn below)
- LAX Theme Building with Los Angeles skyline and downtown traffic
- Hotel Del Coronado across the bay from San Diego
- One of the 21 missions
- Hot air balloons
- A surfer

- Palm trees and eucalyptus, which are not native to California
- Flying fish
- Breaching whale
- Starfish

Photos by Debbie Smith

TREASURE & TRIVIA

The drive-through tree is a tribute to the famous Wawona Tunnel Tree at Yosemite National Park. It existed from 1881 to 1969 when it was felled by winter storms. There are still a couple of drive-through trees left in the coastal redwoods. The most famous is the Chandelier Tree in Leggett.

LESSON TO LEARN

Catalina Casino, the building in Avalon, is called a casino, but it does not have gambling. Casino is used in its traditional sense as a "place of gathering" or "place of entertainment."

TREASURE & TRIVIA

Hotel Del Coronado was used as an exterior model for the Grand Floridian Hotel in Walt Disney World in Florida. The "Hotel Del" also has a famous movie history.

See if you can identify the following in the mural to the right as you enter Disney's California Adventure:

- California state flag (bear with red star)
- deer
- snow skier
- sea otters
- grapes
- Hwy 1 near San Simeon
- Monterey cypress
- Lombard Street in San Francisco
- Victorian homes of San Francisco
- San Francisco Presidio
- Chinatown and Chinese dragon
- Palace of Fine Arts in San Francisco
- San Francisco skyline including the Transamerica Building

Golden Gate Bridge at DCA was a unique solution to a problem. Since 1959, the monorail track has run through the area formerly designed as the parking lot. Moving the track would be very expensive, not practical, and not easy to move. Instead, the Imagineers created a trestle-type effect by creating the Golden Gate Bridge for the monorail to glide through. Since the Golden Gate's purpose here is to enhance the track, this model was not designed to any particular scale of its original. It is beautiful to look at and a great place to have a photo taken.

Incidentally, the towers stand 58' tall here. It's important to note that although you can see the monorail, you cannot board it anywhere inside Disney's California Adventure. There are two monorail stops, one

Photo by Debbie Smith

in Downtown Disney and the other in Tomorrowland inside Disneyland Park. You must have a ticket or pass to enter Disneyland Park to ride the monorail.

Guests entering Disney's California Adventure are greeted with California derived music. The soundtrack playfully reminds you of many California song references.

TREASURE & TRIVIA

The real Golden Gate Bridge divides the Pacific Ocean and the San Francisco Bay. This span was named the Golden Gate Strait back in 1846. Designed by Joseph B. Strauss, the bridge was a $27 million project. Irving F. Morrow and his wife, Gertrude C. Morrow, were credited as the consulting architects who gave the bridge its Art Deco theme. Painted "orange vermillion" or "international orange," the bridge is 1.7 miles long and 90' wide. There is a suspension of 1.2 miles and the bridge sits 200' above the water. The towers are 500' above the roadway. The Golden Gate Bridge weighs 419,800 tons. Construction began on the bridge January 5, 1933, and it opened to pedestrians on May 27, 1937. The following day, the Golden Gate Bridge officially opened at 12 noon to vehicles, ahead of schedule and under budget. The Golden Gate Bridge won the second position as the Top 10 Construction Achievements of the 20th century by CONEXPO-CON/AGG.

Disney Urban Legend:

In the early days, Disney's California Adventure had two versions of its music for opening the Park. In the song *Feels Alright* there was a version that went, "Hope you enjoy everything under the sun," on warm, sunny days. On cloudy days, the lyrics were changed to say, "Hope you enjoy a new state of fun."

Although the rest of the songs are mostly from the 1960s, see if you can pick up any of these tunes:

San Fernando Valley—written by Gordon Jenkins and sang by Bing Crosby

Hooray for Hollywood—which appropriately has a line in the song that says, "with any luck you could be Donald Duck" by Richard Whiting (1938)

California Dreamin' by The Mamas & the Papas

I Love LA by Randy Newman

California, Here I Come sang by Al Jolson

California Girls by The Beach Boys

Little Old Lady from Pasadena by Jan & Dean

Do you Know the Way to San Jose by Dionne Warwick

Hollywood Nights by Bob Seger

San Francisco Bay Blues by Peter, Paul & Mary

Avalon by Natalie Cole

Route 66 by Natalie Cole

If You're Going to San Francisco (Wear Flowers In Your Hair) by Scott McKenzie

26 Miles (Santa Catalina) by The Four Preps

Surf City by Jan & Dean

Surfin' USA by The Beach Boys

TREASURE & TRIVIA

Both *Avalon* and *Route 66* were sung by Nat "King" Cole and his daughter Natalie Cole.

The theme park experience is designed to trigger your senses. Your eyes have a lot to look at, and your ears are filled with California music. Repeat visitors to Disney's California Adventure are very familiar with the French roasted coffee smell drifting by. Although guests believe that the aroma is drifting in from Baker's Field Bakery, the fragrance is so strong that it's most likely a little Imagineer magic at work gently reminding you where you can purchase a cup of joe.

Disneyland was built before the creation of the Hidden Mickey. But Disney's California Adventure was built as the phenomenon was growing strong; Imagineers had a lot of fun adding Hidden Mickeys in Disney's California Adventure. If you're in a contest to find the most Hidden Mickeys, you should do most of your hunting in the shops. Almost every store has a Hidden Mickey to seek out. Since the merchandise is often changed, don't

Photo by Debbie Smith

focus on what you can purchase in each of the stores, but rather the permanent display fixtures.

Greetings from California Shop

The exterior of Greetings from California blend with the surrounding areas, which forces this façade to blend the various styles. For example, the entrance sign above the Golden Gate Bridge looks like a giant postcard, tying in with the murals and entrance plaza. The store entrances facing the plaza have decorative features that are similar to those found on the buildings in Hollywood and tie in with the Hollywood Pictures Backlot next door.

The rooms in Greetings from California are themed to various areas of California and DCA. The rooms from the main gate entrance

TREASURE & TRIVIA

Notice the silver globe above the corner on the far entrance to the Greetings from California store. The globe is based on the spire found at Crossroads of the World, a shopping center in Hollywood. Another replica can be found at Disney-MGM Studios in Walt Disney World in Florida, except the Disney-MGM Studios globe has a Mickey on top that doubles as a lightning rod.

Photo by Debbie Smith

to the Sunshine Plaza are in the following order:

Forest Room (Grizzly Peak Recreation Area) As you enter the forest room, if you look back at the entrance, you'll see you've just walked through a drive-through tree. There is also a quote from John Muir at the top of one of the display shelves. "The clearest way into a universe is through a forest wilderness."

Beach Room (Paradise Pier) The tops of the display shelves have metal signs with the names of California beaches and bays.

HIDDEN MICKEY

In a mural with Mickey and Minnie enjoying the beach, notice a Hidden Mickey in the lower right-hand corner as a shadow in the sand.

LESSON TO LEARN

John Muir was born April 21, 1838, in Scotland. He moved to the United States in 1849, schooled at the University of Wisconsin and visited Yosemite Valley for the first time in 1868. He moved to California and is known as one of the earliest modern preservationists. Muir is the founder of the Sierra Club and camped in Yosemite with President Theodore Roosevelt. During Roosevelt's visit, Muir persuaded the president to protect the country's natural resources. His activism saved Yosemite Valley and other places in the northwest. John Muir's likeness is on the 2005 California quarter. Muir died December 24, 1894, in Los Angeles after visiting his daughter. It was said that he died of a broken heart, as the Hetch Hetchy Valley dam was signed into law by Woodrow Wilson. Just a year earlier Muir's efforts to stop the dam failed. John Muir wrote several books during his lifetime, including one that is still popular today, *The Mountains of California*, written in 1894. His home and ranch in Martinez, Calif., is an historic site.

Photo by Kendra Trahan

HIDDEN MICKEY

Directly across from the Mickey and Minnie mural is another mural. This time it's Goofy and Pluto playing at the beach. A Hidden Mickey can be seen in the shadow in the sand. Notice the Hidden Mickey in front of Goofy.

Underwater Room The ceiling is wavy and made to simulate the ocean surface.

HIDDEN MICKEY

There is a painting near the photo cashier area with Goofy scuba diving. Look for a Hidden Mickey in the bubbles.

HIDDEN MICKEY

Mickey Mouse is wearing swim trunks with a Hidden Mickey logo on the stripe of his swim trunks.

DCA Room (in General) This room has stylized logos of some of the Park's opening day attractions.

Traffic and Street Scene Room This area has fun street signs, such

as "Monorail Crossing" as it goes through the Golden Gate Bridge. There are also billboards featuring the Disney Fab 5 (Mickey, Minnie, Donald, Goofy, Pluto).

Hollywood Room
(Hollywood Pictures Backlot)

HIDDEN MICKEY

There is an oversized camera hanging on the walls inside the center of the Greetings from California gift shop. Notice the dot in the center of the light bulb. It's a very subtle Hidden Mickey.

Poppy Fields

TREASURE & TRIVIA

The candy shop is filled with decorative flowers. This flower is the California poppy, the state flower.

Sunshine Plaza Hub
The Sunshine Plaza has a 60-foot-high titanium-clad sun sculpture above a wave fountain. The huge sun icon is inlaid with tiny bits of glass that reflect sunlight off six high-tech heliostatic mirrors that bounce rays from the sun onto the reflective surfaces of the icon. The six mirrors

Photo by Debbie Smith

rotate to follow the sun throughout the day. Guests who take a few moments to rest in the Sunshine Plaza hub will notice the fountain at the base of the sun sculpture creates several different kinds of waves.

Directly in front of the sun sculpture is the dedication plaque. It reads very similarly to the dedication of Disneyland. For comparison, I've put the two side by side so you can see.

Photo by Debbie Smith

Photo by Debbie Smith

"To all who believe in the power of dreams . . . Welcome! Disney's California Adventure opens its golden gates to you. Here we pay tribute to the dreamers of the past . . . the native people, explorers, immigrants, aviators, entrepreneurs and entertainers who built the Golden State. And we salute a new generation of dreamers who are creating the wonders of tomorrow . . . from the silver screen to the computer screen . . . from the fertile farmlands to the far reaches of space. Disney's California Adventure celebrates the richness and diversity of California . . . its land, its people, its spirit and above all, the dreams that it continues to inspire."

—Michael Eisner

🖐 HIDDEN MICKEY

Give yourself bonus points for finding this Hidden Mickey; it is harder than most. Go directly to the dedication plaque under the sun and wave pool. Notice that there are stripes in the pavement with more glass than the regular cement sections. Count three stripes to the right of the plaque facing the wave pool. The Hidden Mickey will be approximately five inches away from that stripe, but approximately 13 feet away from the bench in front of the wave pool. It is not in glass, but stamped and discolored in the concrete.

To all who come to this happy place—Welcome! Disneyland is your land. Here age relives fond memories of the past . . . and here youth may savor the challenge and promise of the future. Disneyland is dedicated to the ideals, the dreams and the hard facts that have created America . . . with the hope that it will be a source of joy and inspiration to the entire world."

—Walt Disney

California Zephyr

Following World War II, millions of travelers came to California from Chicago via the California Zephyr. This is one of the original F7 diesel locomotive California Zephyr engines built by General Motors Electro-Motive Division. It was transported by a flatbed truck from Illinois. The rest of the cars are replicas of the train with clever store openings cut from the cars.

Photo by: Debbie Smith

Photo by Debbie Smith

TREASURE & TRIVIA

The California Zephyr (a.k.a. "Silver Lady") was a state-of-the-art train back in 1949. The route from Chicago to San Francisco opened March 20, 1949, and traveled 2,525 miles in two-and-a-half days. It originally had five dome cars like the one used as the entry to Engine Ear Toys. The California Zephyr trains stopped running March 22, 1970, although the passenger route is still in use today. The route is still called the California Zephyr. The Zephyr was originally run by the Chicago, Burlington, and Quincy (CB&Q or "Burlington Route"); the Denver and Rio Grande Western ("Rio Grande") and the Western Pacific. Western Pacific ran the train on the California portion of the route. A train with the same name was re-established by Amtrak in 1983 and continues to run, although the route is modified from the original California Zephyr route.

TREASURE & TRIVIA

You may notice that each of the cars on the California Zephyr has a name beginning with "Silver." For example the "Engine-Ears Toys" has a train car named "Silver Crescent." Keeping up with the original partnership of CB&Q rail lines, all stainless steel cars were named with the preceding word "silver." During its 20-year career of taking passengers through the scenic journey through Denver, Salt Lake and Sacramento, the California Zephyr used 77 "silver" names for its cars. Imagineers didn't have to work their magic for the "Silver Platter" dining car. That is the actual name of the dining car, which is also fitting for Baker's Field Bakery.

TREASURE & TRIVIA

Imagineers cleverly named the Baker's Field Bakery after the city of Bakersfield. Bakersfield is approximately 140 miles northeast of Anaheim.

TREASURE & TRIVIA

Go inside the Baker's Field Bakery and Bur-r-r Bank Ice Cream to see wall displays with historic train china, advertisements and other paper goods from the California Zephyr. There are photographs by railroad photographer Robert Morris. There are also Western Pacific employee magazines and a timetable. Behind the counter of Bur-r-r Bank Ice Cream are posters and more photos of the California Zephyr. Baker's Field Bakery has a mural of the Zephyr traveling through the mountains of California. Notice the engine nose is 804-A, the same train as the one the bakery is in. The bakery is hosted by Nescafé and features their products.

Photo by Debbie Smith

Photo by Debbie Smith

TREASURE & TRIVIA

Bur-r-r Bank Ice Cream is named after the city of Burbank, Calif. Burbank is about 36 miles north of Anaheim and the headquarters and studios for the Walt Disney Company. Bur-r-r Bank Ice Cream is hosted by Nestlé Ice cream.

The buildings around the California Zephyr pay tribute to the Mission-style architecture used in several California historic railroad stations, such as Los Angeles Union Station, the San Diego Santa Fe Depot and the Glendale Railroad Station, all of which are still in use by Amtrak. For example, the pattern on the dome on the information booth is similar to one found on the twin domes of the San Diego Santa Fe Depot. The chandeliers above the counter at Baker's Field Bakery are similar to those found in the 1939 Los Angeles Union Station waiting room. The clam shell designs over the doorways of Bur-r-r Bank Ice Cream are similar to designs found above the doors at Los Angeles Union Station and the Glendale depot.

Engine-Ears Toys: While the interior of Baker's Field Bakery and Bur-r-r Bank Ice Cream are meant to pay tribute to real-life stations, the interior of Engine-Ears Toys conveys a more childlike motif, with a display that looks like a steam train and wall displays that are based on greatly simplified versions of train station designs. The walls past the California Zephyr replica cars show a more 19th century "gingerbread" style, like Frontierland Station in Disneyland. The walls opposite the California Zephyr cars show a more Mission-style influence. In particular, note the tower near the caboose of the train display shelf. It's a representation of the clock tower at Los Angeles Union Station.

Photo by Debbie Smith

The Hyperion Theater is modeled after the Los Angeles Theater built in 1930-1931.

Chapter 3

Hollywood Pictures
BACKLOT

Walt Disney once considered giving guests a studio tour, but space was limited and guests would disrupt the filming process. Instead, Walt made a film, released in 1941, called *The Reluctant Dragon*, which gave a tour of the Disney Studios. The backstage tour, the old glamour of Hollywood and the mystique of how television shows and movies are made inspired the idea behind Hollywood Pictures Backlot. The concept for building a Hollywood set and recognizing the rich history in film and television is a natural for Disney's California Adventure.

Many of the attractions in this area of the Park are recycled from Walt Disney World, most

TREASURE & TRIVIA

Many guests think that Hollywood Pictures Backlot is referenced primarily to the city of Hollywood. Actually there was a Division of the Walt Disney Company called Hollywood Pictures that produced films that were oriented to more adult interests. The executives announced the formation of Hollywood Pictures on December 1, 1988, and by February of 1989 it began operations with its first film *Arachnophobia*, released in 1990. Hollywood Pictures produced these familiar titles among others: *The Hand that Rocks the Cradle*, *Medicine Man*, *Straight Talk*, *Encino Man*, *The Distinguished Gentleman*, *Swing Kids*, *The Joy Luck Club*, *Tombstone*, *Quiz Show*, *Mr. Holland's Opus*, *While You Were Sleeping* and *Dangerous Minds*. In 1996 Hollywood Pictures ended its producing role, but its label is still used for distribution.

Photo by Debbie Smith

specifically Disney's-MGM Studios, which opened in May of 1989. Michael Eisner supported the idea of Walt Disney World's third theme park built as an operating movie, television and animation studio. Walt understood filming with tourists around would be difficult. Today, Disney's-MGM Studios is less like a working studio and more like a theme park. Disney's California Adventure took some of the most popular attractions Disney's-MGM Studios had to offer and left the filming up in Burbank. Perhaps because Disneyland already had some of the other attractions also at Disney's-MGM Studios, such as Star Tours, Indiana Jones-themed attraction and Fantasmic!, DCA didn't need to allocate as much land to it.

Hollywood Pictures Backlot is designed to celebrate all that is good and fun about tinseltown. Even the street glitters. You can learn a little about animation, see some theater, enter an episode of *The Twilight Zone* or maybe spot a celebrity. The area uses classic Los Angeles architecture for inspiration. The main street is called Hollywood Boulevard, just like in the Disney's-MGM Studio's Park.

The funny storefronts are puns to famous Hollywood movies and historic buildings in town. Many of the buildings are inspired by the art deco and Spanish-style façades, like The Pantages Theatre and El Capitan Theatre, both owned by the Walt Disney Company. The El Capitan façade usually has the most recent Disney film posted in lights.

TREASURE & TRIVIA

Why are there elephants at the entrance? The elephant gateway was inspired by a set that director D.W. Griffith built right in the middle of Hollywood Boulevard in 1916. In keeping with Griffith's "Babylonian" design, the Backlot elephant towers are etched with hieroglyphics and fitted with Arabian ornamental lights. These elephants stand just 11 feet tall compared to the 50-foot originals.

TREASURE & TRIVIA

The original elephants in Hollywood were part of a set from the 1916 film *Intolerance* by D.W. Griffith. They once stood at the corner of Hollywood and Sunset. It was once considered the most famous set in history because when Griffith finished filming, he left the elephants standing at the intersection. Over the years, the elephants eroded and were removed, but today if you go to the corner of Highland and Hollywood at the Kodak Theatre you'll see a reproduction of them in the shopping complex. Look for the elephants next time you watch the Oscars.

Photo by Debbie Smith

LESSON TO LEARN

D.W. Griffith is often called the father of the motion picture. He was born January 22, 1875, in Crestwood, Ky. He left there in 1897, to pursued a career in acting and writing for theater. He eventually took a job with American Biograph Company, where he directed over 450 short films and experimented with storytelling techniques. He was the first director to fully realize the medium's potential and is credited for inventing such cinematic devices as the iris shot, the mask, crosscutting and flashbacks. His major epics were *The Birth of a Nation* (1915), and *Way Down East* (1920). Griffith never achieved monumental success again and was forced to retire in 1931. In 1935, he was awarded an Oscar for his contributions to the art of motion pictures. Griffith died in Los Angeles in 1948.

HIDDEN MICKEY

Unlike the elephants in Hollywood, the platform beneath the elephants has a Hidden Mickey. Look in between the two lions facing each other.

Admire some of the classic Los Angeles architecture and enjoy some of the storefront puns. For more information on the actual buildings that inspired the look of Hollywood Pictures Backlot go to appendix D.

Award Wieners
"Best Wiener in a Supporting Roll."
Imagineers are having a little fun with the many award shows that take place in Hollywood. Actually, Los Angeles has a famous hot dog stand called Pink's. It started as a stand in 1939 and has served many celebrities. In fact the celebrity photos line the walls.

Philip A. Couch Casting Agency
A little inside joke about the infamous "Casting Couches."

Gone with the Chin, Plastic Surgery Center.
Dr. Nipantuck, "We never tell."
Here's a playful dig about commonplace plastic surgery in Los Angeles and a reference to *Gone with the Wind*, by Margaret Mitchell. The 1939 film starred Vivian Leigh and Clark Gable and is one of the most popular films of all time.

The Souvenir Itch
This is a playful reference to a great place to buy keepsakes and a tease to the 1955 film *The Seven Year Itch*, starring Marilyn Monroe.

TREASURE & TRIVIA

You may notice the structure is named Cahuenga Building. The Campo de Cahuenga is the birthplace of California. Although this building looks nothing like ancient adobe recreated in the 1950's, visitors can tour the Park where negotiations were settled to end the Mexican-American war on January 13, 1847.

Schmoozies

A great place to get smoothies. Hollywood perfected the art of schmoozing to coax difficult actors, both male and female, to perform. Although the collages on the Schmoozies building look like a nesting ground for Hidden Mickeys there are no true Mickeys in the collage. The collages are made of china and the themes represent areas of California. Look for interesting pieces.

Photo by Debbie Smith

Photo by Debbie Smith

Fairfax Market

Referring to what is known today as the original farmer's market. In 1934, a group of farmers pulled their trucks onto an empty lot on the corner of Third and Fairfax in Los Angeles and began selling their produce off their tailgates. Customers quickly arrived and began to purchase fruit, vegetables and flowers. Soon it became a central meeting place for Angelenos. It remains a tourist attraction in Southern California today, although the complex has expanded and been reconstructed several times. Walt Disney was known for hanging out at the Fairfax Market on occasion.

Argyle Building

Referring to The Argyle Hotel on Sunset Boulevard designed by architect Leland A. Bryant in 1929. The Argyle Hotel is known for its Art Deco styling and proximity to the famous nightclubs of the 1930s and 1940s. Former residents include Howard Hughes, John Wayne and Bugsy Siegel. The original Argyle

Hotel has appeared in many films, such as *Wayne's World II*, *Get Shorty*, *The Player* and *The Italian Job*. The building is considered one of the most important Art Deco structures in Los Angeles and is listed on the National Register of Historic Places. Locals still consider it a hot spot.

Ben Hair, an Epic Salon

A little jab at the 1959 film *Ben-Hur* starring Charlton Heston.

La Brea Carpets
"You'll dig our rugs."

This play on words is directed at the La Brea tar pits found in the heart of Los Angeles.

LESSON TO LEARN

What became known as the La Brea tar pits was first discovered in 1769 during the Portola expedition. It is a large marsh of tar that boils and bubbles. It is considered the first indication that there was oil in western America. Between 1906 and 1915, thousands of ice age fossils were recovered from the pits; more than one million bones have been recovered. The George C. Page Museum of La Brea Discoveries sits adjacent to the tar pits and is open to the public. It houses many of the major finds from the tar pits.

Dial M for Muscle workout

A reference to the 1954 Alfred Hitchcock film *Dial M for Murder*. This film starred Grace Kelly and Robert Cummings. One year after filming *Dial M for Murder*, Bob Cummings would be one of the three television hosts at the opening of Disneyland. Do you know who the other two hosts were?

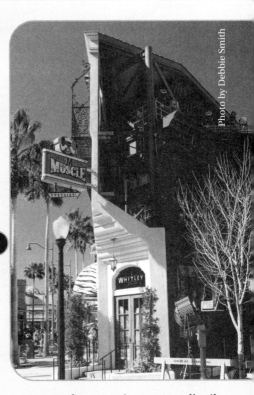

Photo by Debbie Smith

LESSON TO LEARN

You may notice at the corner of DCA's Sunset and Hollywood streets that the Whitley building is only half finished. Unlike typical Disney fashion, Walt always designed the buildings to appear complete from the "on-stage" view. But since this is Hollywood Pictures Backlot, the buildings are designed to look like movie sets. Movie sets use a lot of façades like this one, where only the camera angle views are finished and the rest of the building is just a shell. This practice saved the filmmakers a lot of money. Later the phrase, "putting on a façade" came into vogue, referring to the false front or image people sometimes portray.

Across the street is a trompe l'oeil of The Beverly building and the El Capitan Theatre. This is a popular photo spot for guests. The Beverly building is loosely modeled after the Wiltern Theatre. The El Capitan is modeled after the El Capitan Theatre, which is owned by Disney. The trompe l'oeil is not completely accurate, but if you were to go back in time to Hollywood you would not see the Kodak Theatre and shopping mall directly across from the El Capitan Theatre and Grauman's Chinese Theatre on the same block. One other major omission to the trompe l'oeil is that the sidewalk should have the Walk of Stars.

Answer: Art Linkletter and Ronald Reagan.

LESSON TO LEARN

Max Factor was born Frank Firestein in St. Louis, Mo., on August 18, 1904. His father, Max Firestein, began the family's business in glamour by opening a wig store in Razan, Russia in the 1890s. In 1904, he emigrated to the United States and opened a perfume, makeup and wig concession at the St. Louis World's Fair. Frank Firestein was born later that same year. In 1908, the family moved to Los Angeles. By 1916, Frank joined his father in business on Hill Street and from there he created a makeup empire. Frank changed his name to Max Factor, Jr. and became head of the company that would make ordinary people into dazzling stars. Max Factor invented the first film makeup, a grease paint that was in a tube, lip gloss, pancake makeup and fake eyelashes. In the 1930 to 1940s Max Factor dominated the makeup industry both in Hollywood and among American women. Because many of his Hollywood clients would appear in glamour magazines, Max Factor was in great demand. His client list included Joan Crawford, Jean Harlow, Claudette Colbert, Bette Davis, Judy Garland, Lucille Ball, Betty Grable, Ginger Rogers and Rita Hayworth, among many others. He even had a few famous male clients such as John Wayne and Frank Sinatra. Max Factor died on June 7, 1996, of congestive heart failure in Los Angeles.

The Max Factor building is now the Hollywood History Museum at 1660 N. Highland Ave., Hollywood, Calif. Here guests can see the four make-up rooms, costumes, movie props and sets. The Max Factor exhibit is only a small part of the museum, which is open Thursday to Sunday from 10 a.m. to 5 p.m. The admission fee is $15 and $2 is credited toward parking.

LESSON TO LEARN

According to the New Oxford Dictionary trompe l' oeil, is "an illusion in art, esp. as used to trick the eye into perceiving a painted detail as a three-dimensional object."

Floral Canyon

This is a fun reference to Laurel Canyon, which separates Beverly Hills to the west from Hollywood to the east.

Sweet Shop Named Desire
Stella, Proprietor

This reference is for the Tennessee Williams movie and play, *A Streetcar Named Desire*.

Leash! Camera! Action!

Directors are known for commanding "Lights! Camera! Action!" Although since the store window looks like a pet store, Leash! Camera! Action! is more appropriate.

Role Models RM

The text of Role Models is written in the scriptive Beverly Hills style. This building is actually designed after the famous Max Factor building. Back in the 1930s and 1940s, potential stars would visit Max Factor and develop a glamour look. Today, Max Factor is known for his makeup line, but in the early Hollywood days, Max Factor was the main glamour makeup artist.

OPENING DAY ATTRACTION

Jim Henson's Muppet Vision 3D

This was an opening day attraction that was dedicated by Charlie Rivkin, president and CEO of Jim Henson Studios, and Cynthia Harris, president of the Disneyland Resort. The attraction was first created for Disney's-MGM Studios in Orlando, Fla. in 1991. Jim Henson produced, directed and voiced Kermit in this attraction. Jim Henson Presents Muppet Vision 3D would prove to be the last production of Jim Henson's illustrious career.

The 3D film is based on the television series *The Muppet Show*, which includes such favorites as Kermit the Frog, Miss Piggy, Gonzo, Fozzie Bear and a new character, Waldo, the spirit of 3D.

The television series *The Muppet Show* aired from 1976 to 1981. This family comedy watched Kermit and his friends put on a variety show. Kermit the Frog is the manager of a vaudeville-style theatre, which regularly has more comedy and drama behind the stage than on it. Kermit has to contend with a wannabe comedian bear, the smothering advances of Miss Piggy, crabby regular theatre patrons and uncontrollable livestock, while greeting and caring for the weekly guest star.

Photo by Debbie Smith

Many top stars made appearances on *The Muppet Show*. All the women made Miss Piggy jealous, and Miss Piggy fell in love with almost every male star. Some celebrities making an appearance on *The Muppet Show* included: Candice Bergen, Jim Nabors, Florence Henderson, Don Knotts, Steve Martin, George Burns, Elton John, Julie Andrews, Bob Hope, Danny Kaye, Sylvester Stallone, Liberace, John Denver, Dudley Moore, Christopher Reeve, Diana Ross, Gladys Knight, Carol Burnett, Gene Kelly and even Disney Legend Wally Boag, famous for the Golden Horseshoe Show at Disneyland.

TREASURE & TRIVIA

As you walk into the building, there is a theater office to your left. First notice that Jim Henson's photograph is there. Then read the "Be Back Soon" sign. It says that the key is under the mat. If you were to walk over to the door to the office, you'll see a mat. Lift the mat and you'll see the key.

HIDDEN MICKEY

In the pre-show area there are some bombs hanging from the ceiling near a light. If you stand directly underneath it, the light makes a head and the bombs make the ears of a Hidden Mickey.

LESSON TO LEARN

J im Henson was the creator of the Muppets and most recognized for Kermit the Frog. The original Kermit was first made in the 1950s out of Jim's mother's overcoat that she had thrown in a trash can. By 1969, a PBS children's show *Sesame Street* made Kermit and his friends part of their regular staff. The Muppets became so popular that they spun off their own half-hour television series and movie-empire beginning with *The Muppet Movie* in 1979. Jim Henson also created *Muppet Babies, Fraggle Rock* and the *Teenage Mutant Ninja Turtle* movie. Tragically, in 1990, Jim Henson was stricken with a rare bacterial infection and died rather suddenly at the age of 53 in a New York hospital. He was preparing to sell his Muppet empire to the Disney Studios. His son Brian took over the studios and kept the Muppets for a while. In 2004, the Muppets were eventually sold to Disney.

TREASURE & TRIVIA

I n the front of the pre-show room, if you look up high you'll see some patriotic soldiers and a colorful cannon on the catwalk. Study the soldiers closely because you'll see them again in the Muppet Vision 3D finale. The soldiers were actually used in the filming of Muppet Vision. The attraction in Florida also has movie prop soldiers in the rafters.

HIDDEN MICKEY

Also in the front of the pre-show room are some eggs in Gonzo's airplane. Some say the eggs create a Hidden Mickey.

TREASURE & TRIVIA

The Imagineers had some fun with the scene clappers on the wall. Puns like "Scene; in all the best places," "Take; Moi," "Take; the A train," and an old favorite, "Take; my wife please."

The pre-show has a clever use of progressive television. Sponsored by Kodak, the pre-show uses three televisions that do not show the same picture, but instead three different views of the room. This is one example that demonstrates the genius of Jim Henson and his comedic timing. There's even a light-hearted spoof at Mickey Mouse and Donald Duck.

HIDDEN MICKEY

In the pre-show film, there is a scene after the maintenance Muppets put up the sponsor signs. It looks like television static and in the center is an unusual Hidden Mickey unusual because his ears are not full circles, but it qualifies as a Hidden Mickey.

LESSON TO LEARN

On the upper far wall of the pre-show room is a series of classic paintings spoofed with Muppet characters. These are reproductions created for a calendar where the Muppet Cast was inserted into famous paintings by great masters. Such care and detail went into the photos that they were exhibited at the Berry-Hill Galleries in New York and published as a book, *Miss Piggy's Treasury of Art Masterpieces from the Kermitage Collection.* These paintings were used in a calendar. Can you identify the names and artists of the true classics?

- The Birth of Venus
  by Sandro Botticelli
- American Gothic
  by Grant Wood
- Blue Boy
  by Thomas Gainsborough
- Arrangement in Grey & Black: The Artist's Mother (Whistler's Mother) by James A. McNeill Whistler
- Henry VIII
  by Hans Holbein

HIDDEN MICKEY

For those who really pay attention, notice that Scooter is wearing a lab coat with a Disney nametag in the pre-show film. The character above his name on the name tag is Mickey Mouse.

The 575-seat theater was custom built especially for the show. Notice the ornamentation of Kermit as producer and director over the doorways and Fozzie Bear as the Greek comedy and drama masks. The bunny named Bean is decorated all over the apron of the stage. The crown of the stage is the likeness of the stars of the show.

The film is 14-1/2 minutes and is the mildest of all the 3D films at Disneyland Resort. (The other 3D films are *Honey I Shrunk the Audience* in Disneyland and *A Bug's Life* also in Disney's California Adventure.) *Muppet Vision 3D* was quite ahead of its time with its special effects that take maximum advantage of the 3D format. Purists would say the film is actually 4D, because the bubbles and water can be touched, unlike the images in the film. Jim Henson directed and starred (as Kermit) in the film and very cleverly used props in the film to enhance the 3D experience. The movie interacts with audio-animatronic characters in the theater, water that's sprayed on the audience, bubbles that fall from the ceiling and the Sweethums character walks out to the audience.

A new character is introduced in Muppet Vision 3D, Waldo the spirit of 3D. Waldo first appeared in a television show called *The Jim Henson Hour* and was digitally created to experiment with computer generated imaging (CGI). To quote Jim Henson in his biography *Jim Henson, The Works* it says that "Waldo is nothing less than the world's first digitized puppet—a character who can be performed by a puppeteer using a remote control rig, but who comes to life via a computer and a color monitor. Waldo is, in other words, a computer-generated image that can be manipulated by a puppeteer much as the figures in a Nintendo game are manipulated with a joystick. This enables the puppet to operate in real time and to interact with other real Muppets." A predecessor to Pixar and the strong user of CGI, Waldo is a pioneer. Consequently, when he turns himself into Mickey Mouse, it is the first time Mickey has ever been filmed in CGI.

 TREASURE & TRIVIA

The Sweethums on screen who bounces a paddle ball directly toward the camera is Jim Henson's younger son John Henson.

Although Disney wouldn't buy the Muppets for many years later, the film has some clues that they were looking to collaborate. Not only does Mickey Mouse appear in CGI, but during Sam the Eagle's finale to "all nations, but mostly America" some characters come out dressed like the "it's a small world" attraction in Disneyland. At the end of the film, Kermit is sitting on a fire truck. Notice the license plate of the truck—it's the Buena Vista logo of the Sleeping Beauty Castle. Buena Vista is also the Walt Disney Company's film distribution company.

HIDDEN MICKEY

At the end of the film, when guests are walking by the hole in the back of the theater, notice that some are carrying Mickey Mouse balloons. Technically, these could count as Hidden Mickeys.

TREASURE & TRIVIA

The Muppet Show theme song was co-written by Jim Henson and Sam Pottle. Many of the *Sesame Street* television show albums have children's songs written by Sam Pottle.

TREASURE & TRIVIA

Statler and Waldorf, the two old men in the balcony of *The Muppet Show*, were named for two five-star hotels in New York.

TREASURE & TRIVIA

The Muppet Fozzie Bear was named after Frank Oz, using his first initial "F" and his last name "Oz" to create the moniker Fozzie. Frank, an actor, director, writer, producer and puppeteer, was known for bringing Miss Piggy, Fozzie and many of the Muppet characters to life.

When the attraction first opened, there was a wonderful Jim Henson reference that has now been painted over. In the photo you'll notice the Muppet Theater, front of the building. Notice the painted faces outside Muppet Vision 3D. This is a special tribute to Jim Henson and the *Jack Paar Show*. The book *Jim Henson, The Works* mentions that in 1964 Jim Henson, Don Sahlin, Jerry Juhl and Frank Oz were in the green room for a 10 a.m. rehearsal. When the Muppets weren't needed until 4 p.m., the

Photo by Debbie Smith

men turned their creative talents to a utilities closet in their dressing room. Don had brought some paints for touch-ups, so they started painting faces on everything. At one point they hopped into a cab to get more supplies from their workshop. News started to get around about what they were doing, and a knock came on the door and a voice outside said, "Hello, I'm Charlton Heston. Could I see your closet?" Since practical jokes were common with the Muppet crew, they yelled back, "Yeah, sure, you're Charlton Heston." Only when he opened the door did they realize it wasn't a joke and Mr. Heston really was standing outside their door. When the host Jack Paar

heard what they had done, he took a camera back into the dressing room to show what the "crazy Muppet people" had done. It is believed that the decorated closet in the NBC Studios in Radio City survives today.

HIDDEN MICKEY

Outside Muppet Vision 3D there is a souvenir shop called Studio Store. On the right-hand side look for three photo frames hung together, creating a Hidden Mickey. It might be easier to see when you stand at the right-side counter looking back toward Muppet Vision 3D.

TREASURE & TRIVIA

The Swedish Chef was inspired by a true person. A Swedish cook by the name of Lars Baeckmann made his first and only appearance on television. Considered a total failure, his appearance showed him hectically preparing some meal and mumbling in English and Swedish. However, the writers of *The Muppet Show* saw it and found it hilarious, inspiring the Swedish Chef to his likeness (including the thick moustache). Baeckmann, who had a traveling cooking show in Sweden, was paid $80 for the rights to the character. He is considered a good cook with a great sense of humor.

TREASURE & TRIVIA

Kermit and friends officially joined the Walt Disney Company when Jim Henson Company sold the Muppets in February 2004.

Monsters Inc!
Mike and Sully to the rescue!

This attraction opened as part of the Disneyland 50th Anniversary celebration on December 20, 2005. The story of *Monsters Inc.* is recreated in this dark ride. If you missed the Disney-Pixar film, the queue sets up the story. Essentially monsters visit the human world using children's closet doors for transportation. Their purpose is to scare kids to create a power source for the city of Monstropolis. The catch: monsters believe that children are toxic and the Child Detection Agency (CDA) protects the city against children. The concern for Monstropolis is that current films, games and television shows are making it more difficult to scare children.

TREASURE & TRIVIA

Monsters are even encouraged to walk to work to save power. Or perhaps "Stalk" as it says in the crosswalk. There are two newspaper stands near the loading queue with the *Monstropolis Horn* and the *Daily Glob* that describe the situation. This is just one detail that Pixar went to the trouble in the film to make: all the fine print in newspapers, posters and flyers, instead of the normal Hollywood gibberish newspapers used in film. It was felt that DVDs would allow children to stop frames and read the fine print. Pixar animators didn't want its viewers to be disappointed.

The attraction uses the former Superstar Limo building with the limos redone to look like taxicabs. Since the Imagineers didn't need to redevelop a ride system, this attraction was better prepared to use multiple types of technology to enhance the ride. There are more than 40 audio-animatronic characters in the attraction, more than any other dark ride.

Rumor has it that Pixar was so impressed with the Imagineer efforts that they enlarged all the commercial posters from the film to be used in the queue. Even the menu at Harry Hausen's restaurant has been replicated.

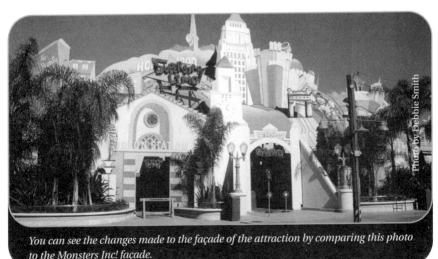

You can see the changes made to the façade of the attraction by comparing this photo to the Monsters Inc! façade.

HIDDEN MICKEY

Left over from the Superstar Limo attraction, there is a Hidden Mickey seen above the skyline as you enter your cab. It is one of the most difficult to find, but if you look at the silhouettes of the buildings between the poles in the bridge, you might find it.

TREASURE & TRIVIA

This is the first Disney attraction that takes guests into a bathroom.

HIDDEN MICKEY

In one of the scenes, Boo is hitting Randall over the head. One of the colors that Randall turns to has a Hidden Mickey; look for the yellow and pink pattern. Incidentally, one of the patterns that Randall turns into is the wallpaper used in the Haunted Mansion. Look for the purple background with lots of eyes.

HIDDEN MICKEY

Just before you enter the CDA cleaning room at the end of the attraction, look at the purple spots on Sully's hip. One is in the shape of a Hidden Mickey.

The license plates on the cabs are quite clever. Which is your favorite?

- BIG FANG
- FOBY AH
- SHRIEK
- 2SCARE U
- GOTCHA
- GROWLR
- FRIGHTN
- 4MONSTR
- PEEKABOO
- WLD THNG
- NO HUMNS

TREASURE & TRIVIA

Superstar Limo was a dark ride where the Monsters Inc. attraction is now. Superstar Limo was an opening day attraction, but also the first attraction to be removed. It had puppets that looked like some recognizable celebrities and were voiced by the actual stars. Inside you would ride a six-person purple limo through Hollywood, where you might spot Joan Rivers, Whoopie Goldberg, Arnold Schwarzenegger and Drew Carey. The attraction was a tribute to modern Hollywood with many icons such as the Grauman's Chinese Theater, the Beverly Hills Hotel and Rodeo Drive.

TREASURE & TRIVIA

The computer-generated animated film *Monsters Inc.* is a Disney and Pixar production. The film was released November 2, 2001, and grossed over $524 million worldwide. The film won an Oscar for Best Original Song "If I Didn't Have You" and was nominated for two other Academy Awards. *Monsters Inc.* was directed by David Silverman and Lee Unkrich. The film used the celebrity voices of Billy Crystal (Mike Wazowski), John Goodman (James P. "Sulley" Sullivan), Steve Buscemi (Randall Boggs) and James Coburn as the CEO Henry J. Waternoose. The premise of the story is to explain why there are monsters in children's closets. The reason? It's their job, as scream generates power for the city of Monstropolis.

TREASURE & TRIVIA

What is the relationship between Pixar and Disney? According to the Corporate Overview for Pixar, in May of 1991 the company entered into a feature film agreement with Walt Disney Pictures for the development and production of up to three animated films to be marketed and distributed by Disney. *Toy Story* was developed, produced and distributed under this agreement. *Toy Story II* would later also fall under this agreement. In February 1997, Pixar entered into a co-production agreement with Disney. Pixar agreed to produce five more original computer animated feature-length films. Disney agreed to co-finance the production, co-own and co-brand the films. Both companies would share equally in the profits and any merchandise. The films under the co-production agreement are *A Bug's Life, Monsters Inc., Finding Nemo, The Incredibles* and *Cars*. The three founding members of Pixar include Steve Jobs, chairman and CEO; Dr. Ed Catmull, president; and John A. Lasseter, executive vice president-Creative. Read more about John Lasseter in "a bug's life chapter" under Flik's Fun Fair. When Bob Iger stepped in as president of the Walt Disney Company, the relationship changed again. Now Pixar is part of the Disney Family.

There are many special effects to appreciate that are new to the dark ride system. Disneyland created the dark ride concept with Peter Pan, Snow White's Scary Adventure and Mr. Toad's Wild Ride back in 1955. This modern version has holograms, computer animation and even the use of ginger scents as you enter the Chinese restaurant and lemon ice as Yeti offers you a snow cone. Each time you ride, a unique experience is created by a couple of effects. In one of the door warehouses, a different scene is created as the door opens and you see where it leads. Sometimes it might be Yeti, other times it might be Randall or someone else altogether. Also, as you finish the ride, Ros will interact with your car by choosing someone and making a response.

Hollywood & Dine

This restaurant is usually closed or used for private functions. Named for the popular Hollywood & Vine cross street in the middle of the theater district.

OPENING DAY ATTRACTION

The Hollywood Backlot Stage

This is an opening day attraction. The stage is primarily used for shows to highlight the Disney characters, with the premise that there is filming on a television or movie set. The show changes frequently but is a good place to get character signatures and rest in the shade.

Photo by Debbie Smith

HIDDEN MICKEY

Near the back lot stage you might see Cruella De Vil's dressing trailer. It is painted white with black spots to look like a Dalmatian. If you walk toward the bathrooms and look on the back side of the trailer, there is a black spot painted as a Hidden Mickey.

Photo by Debbie Smith

Photo by Debbie Smith

OPENING DAY ATTRACTION

Hyperion Theater

The Hyperion was an opening day attraction, but the show inside has changed from time to time.

The first show to appear there was "Disney's Steps in Time," which featured 34 singers and dancers in a 25-minute show that paid tribute to the musical heritage of Disney animation and film. Soon after, a series of other shows including "Blast" appeared there, until "Disney's Aladdin—A Musical Spectacular" settled in.

The Hyperion Theater is the first Broadway-style theater ever built in a Disney theme park. The theater can house an audience of 2,000 people; it's 76 feet tall, while the tower is 90 feet tall. The stage is 55 feet deep, 60 feet wide with 30-foot wings on each side. There are three seating levels with the orchestra at the lowest level, mezzanine the next level higher and the balcony at the top. The theater is a mixture of modern technology with traditional styling. Modern theaters show all the rigging and lighting, where traditional theaters made every effort to hide it. The Hyperion Theater uses an iron mesh to cover, but not completely hide, the lighting.

TREASURE & TRIVIA

The name Hyperion is special to the Disney Company. The Walt Disney Studios moved to 2719 Hyperion Ave. in Los Angeles in 1926. It is where the Mickey Mouse cartoons were drawn and where *Snow White and the Seven Dwarfs* was produced. On May 6, 1940, Walt moved his studios to a bigger lot in Burbank, but he took some of the Hyperion building with him. In the 1960s the Hyperion studio was replaced with a supermarket, where one still stands today. Hyperion is also the name of the Disney Publishing Company.

HIDDEN MICKEY

Inside the Hyperion Theater there are several doors with colorful mesh-like frames. At the mezzanine and balcony levels, look for a large circle in the top center above the door with some smaller circles in a swirl pattern to create a Hidden Mickey.

The production of the *Aladdin* stage show is inspired by the 1992 animated feature by the same name. Aladdin is a young, poor, street-smart kid who falls in love with the Sultan's daughter. When he

 TREASURE & TRIVIA

Aladdin is an Arabian Night story once told by Sherazad, a woman who saved her own life by telling the king and his court a different story every night. It is said that she had 1,000 stories and knew how to develop a cliff hanger so that the King would spare her life another day so he could hear the rest of her story the next evening. Disney's animated film *Aladdin* debuted in a special release on November 11, 1992. Directed by John Musker and Ron Clements, the film casts Robin Williams as the Genie (voice), Jonathan Freeman as the voice of Jafar and Gilbert Gottfried as the voice of Iago. The film idea was originally proposed by Howard Ashman and Alan Menken in 1988 while they were working on *The Little Mermaid.* After Howard Ashman died in 1991, Tim Rice came aboard and wrote "A Whole New World," which won the film an Academy Award for "Best Song." Ashman and Menken also won Oscars for "Best Original Score." Domestically the film grossed $200 million and spun off a children's show and two straight-to-video sequels.

finds a magical lamp that will give him three wishes, his adventure begins. The live stage show has 18 scene changes, 250 costumes for a cast of 50 in 29 different roles. The Genie is the star of the show using pantomime and special effects. Take the time, because you won't want to miss Disney's Aladdin—A Musical Spectacular.

Twilight Zone Tower of Terror

This attraction opened in May of 2004 in DCA, but was created for the Disney-MGM Studios Park in Florida ten years earlier, opening July 21, 1994. While the attraction is a thrill ride, not everyone can handle the fast elevator drop. If you can endure the drop at least once, try because the story and special effects you experience on the attraction equal the thrill of a dropping elevator. The Hollywood Tower Hotel building that houses the Twilight Zone Tower of Terror is designed in the Pueblo Deco architectural style. Pueblo Deco blends elements from the Southwest, Mission and Art Deco styles. The Disney-MGM counterpart in Florida

has two elevator shafts, where the California version has three to increase capacity per hour. The California tower is 183 feet tall and the tallest building at the Disneyland Resort as well as Anaheim.

Photo by Debbie Smith

Notice how quickly the Hollywood Tower Hotel changes to the Twilight Zone.

The Imagineers created the elevator drop with the Twilight Zone story overlay. Many people may remember the eerie and suspenseful television series that ran from 1957 to 1964. The series won two Emmys and was a launching pad for many Hollywood stars such as William Shatner, Robert Redford, Dennis Hopper and many more. Through re-runs the television series has become a pop culture icon for generations. The Imagineers went to great lengths to find and get actual footage of Serling in the pre-show you see in the attraction. For the Sci-Fi and trivia buffs, the Hollywood Tower Hotel is filled with dozens of television props and references to the show. As a teaser, look in the library for an envelope tucked in the book case; it simply says "Rod Serling."

The California tower is supposedly younger, built in 1928, not 1917 like the Florida version. Both towers were inspired for their outer design by the Los Angeles City Hall. (The same building seen in television series such as *Dragnet, Adam 12,* and *Superman* as he leaps over a tall building . . .) Imagineer Cory Sewelson worked on both towers, but the California one has more Pueblo Deco styling.

To keep guests coming back the Imagineers programmed the drop sequence to change periodically. The drop lasts about two seconds, although it seems like a lot longer.

In most cases the elevator makes multiple drops although not always from the 13th floor.

TREASURE & TRIVIA

Rod Edward Serling was the creator of *The Twilight Zone* television series which aired 156 episodes. Rod was born in Syracuse, New York, on December 25, 1924. He died in June 1975 of complications from a coronary bypass surgery.

A two-hour television show was created to tell the Disney Myth behind the haunting of the hotel. "Tower of Terror" aired on October 26, 1997, on *The Wonderful World of Disney* and starred Steve Guttenberg and a young Kirsten Dunst. Copies of the show along with original *Twilight Zone* episodes are often available in the gift shop. Using the characters seen in the attraction, the television show references the Tip Top Club where a Halloween party on the top floor takes place.

The Myth of the Twilight Zone Tower of Terror

On October 31, 1939, the Hollywood Tower Hotel was struck by lightning. An entire guest wing along with an elevator with five occupants disappeared, believed to be sent directly into the Twilight Zone. All the people in the hotel, including those in the lobby disappeared. All that remains is luggage, toys, cards and other accessories just as their owners were in mid-stream of using them. Fearful that disrupting the lobby will affect whether the hotel will recover from the incident, cobwebs and dust layer the room. Today when guests visit the hotel, the television in the library explains the hotel's tragic history. Brave persons willing to visit the twilight zone are invited to ride the service elevators and experience their own journey into another dimension.

Look for a reference to the Tip Top Club before you enter the gift shop. Also notice the name Anthony Fremont; for more information on Anthony Fremont, check out Appendix B. If the library doesn't feel eerie enough, the boiler room will help dampen the mood. Even for guests who don't like the thrill ride of the elevator, they can enjoy the library and exit at the boiler room. Keep in mind that in great Disney Fashion, the elevator ride is more than just the thrill of falling, but more special effects as guests experience more of the Twilight Zone.

There are a couple more differences between the Florida and California versions of "Tower of Terror." The California attraction begins with the elevator already in the position in the drop shaft, where the attraction in Florida must move along a track to get into position. The effect in Florida is amazing as people don't expect an elevator to move forward. Although both attractions have a lot of props and references to the television show, the California attraction is riddled with many more references.

 TREASURE & TRIVIA

As you walk to the left library notice the back door to the hotel front desk has a 22 on it. *Twenty Two* is the name of an episode where a woman has a recurring dream about room 22, which in the hospital is the morgue.

As mentioned, there are so many references to the television show that if you weren't familiar with the show or not interested in it, the references could go on for quite a few pages. Instead it was decided that all the Twilight Zone Television props would be created in a single list at the back of this book. Look to Appendix B to track them all.

HIDDEN MICKEY

This Hidden Mickey is not really hidden, but it is easy to spot and frequently missed. As you watch the film in the library, look at the doll that the little girl is carrying when she enters the elevator. You'll see her carrying the same doll during the attraction.

TREASURE & TRIVIA

Imagineers go so far in telling the story that there are at least two examples of the detail that make the experience as real as possible. When you've seen the library and are waiting to board the service elevator on the ground floor, you'll walk past a workman's desk. His calendar says October 31, 1939, Tuesday, and you'll see the *Los Angeles Examiner* paper on the desk has the same date. Without coincidence, Halloween in 1939 was in fact on Tuesday!

HIDDEN MICKEY

Once you're on the elevator and the show begins, look at the scroll work in the center of the beam on the ceiling of the ghost hallway. A Hidden Mickey is in the center of the painted scroll work.

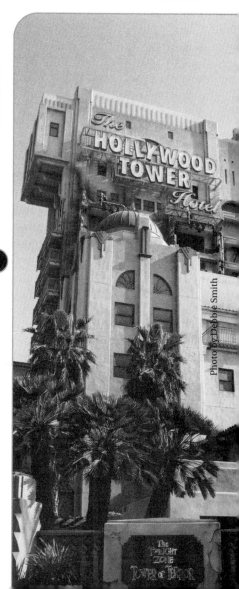

Photo by Debbie Smith

Although not an exact replica it's a nice tribute to the Walt Disney Studio sign at Hyperion Avenue.

TREASURE & TRIVIA

As you walk back toward the Hyperion Theater from The Tower of Terror, you may notice a large sign on the building on the left side that says, "Walt Disney Studios Mickey Mouse and Silly Symphony Sound Cartoons." This is a replica of the sign that once graced the Walt Disney Studio at 2725 Hyperion Ave. in the 1930s. A Gelson's Supermarket is in the current location.

OPENING DAY ATTRACTION

Disney Animation

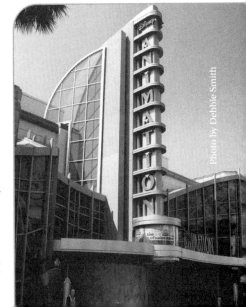

One of the highlights of Hollywood Pictures Backlot is the Animation Building. Not only is the building beautiful, but it also houses several attractions where guests can learn about the animation process. The building is a 40,000-square-foot rectangular box with a couple of theaters, a gallery, a lobby, a store and an interactive walk-through attraction. As you walk through the building, the shape of the building

Animation is the foundation of the Walt Disney Company.   It's very fitting that this attraction is a tribute to its rich animation heritage.

is lost due to the curvilinear shapes and forms that sweep you from one attraction to the other. Dennis Tanida, one of the concept architects, worked with a team to create a feeling of motion and fluid lines like animation itself.

The curved façade has etched glass windows that light up 80 different Disney characters. The hallway winds around to create a full presentation of the Animation Courtyard Gallery.

Animation Courtyard Gallery has larger than life glimpses of the 70 years of Disney animation on suspended projection screens. To the animation admirer, the soundtrack

and colorful, larger than life images, surround you and create an experience that is pure exhilaration. Many different styles of artwork are necessary to create a single full-length animated film, and storyboards, scenery layouts, characters and their development are projected film by film in chronological order. Disney Animation show producer Lori Coltrin describes the Animation Courtyard like this: "The images that surround you depict the world of characters and the movies they come from. Often featured on the screens are backgrounds from films, so you'll be completely immersed in the world of *Bambi*, for instance, with a few characters to help complete the scene. Then, on video screens, we feature character development art, early storyboard art and all the phases that the artists go through as well as clips from the final films."

In the lobby there are 16 screens; the films were originally shown in the order by which they were released, but later changed to show a more random order with old mixed in with newer films. There are colorful perimeter lights in white, red, green and blue that set the mood for each film. The use of surround sound, multiple (6) projectors re-create some of the greatest moments in Disney animation film.

Turtle Talk with Crush—Here you

enter the aqua-torium and get a chance to meet face to face with the sea turtle Crush from the Disney Pixar film *Finding Nemo*. Crush makes an appearance about every 30 minutes. Children are asked to sit up front on the carpet and "parental units" are encouraged to use the seats. Crush engages the kids by using his surfer-dude language and interacts with the children in the audience. This is a great instance of technology used, not for the sake of technology, but story telling. The concepts are relatively simple, but the effect causes people to walk out of there asking, "How did they do that?"

The moonfish help with the

safety messages, Dori, or "little blue," makes an appearance and Crush shares some interesting facts about sea turtles.

Since opening day of DCA this theater has seen a few changes. When the Park opened the nine-minute film *Back to Neverland* starring Walter Cronkite and Robin Williams was featured. *Back to Neverland* was originally created for the opening of Disney's- MGM Studios in Florida. For Walt's 100th Anniversary of his birthday, the film changed to *One Man's Dream*. The theater has 230 seats and was once designed to look like a plush movie studio screening room. The Turtle Talk Rehab was an expensive but much loved upgrade.

TREASURE & TRIVIA

Finding *Nemo* was released by Disney-Pixar in 2003. Directed and written by Andrew Stanton. The co-director was Lee Unkrich. It's a father-son story about a boy clownfish who is stolen from his coral reef home. His father searches the ocean to find him in this underwater adventure. Sadly, Nemo is not in the ocean, but a dentist's office fish tank in Sydney, Australia. The father was voiced by Albert Brooks, who meets up with a forgetful fish, Dori, voiced by Ellen DeGeneres.

LESSON TO LEARN

There are seven different species of sea turtles: green sea turtle, black sea turtle, loggerhead, hawksbill, flat back, kemp ridley and leatherback. Crush is a green sea turtle whose species typically grows to 31 to 44 inches long and can grow to 150 to 410 lbs. Green sea turtles usually feed on sea grass and algae, but there are species of sea turtles that are carnivorous (meat eating), herbivorous (plant eating) and omnivorous (both meat and plant eating). The female may lay 50 to 200 eggs in a single "clutch," but 90% will be lost to predators since the eggs are usually laid in the sand near the shore or in shallow water. Fish, dogs, seabirds, raccoons and ghost crabs all prey on the hatchlings. The female may lay 1 to 9 clutches per season, but mates only every 2 to 3 years. In the film *Finding Nemo*, Nemo asks the question, "How old can a sea turtle live?" Actually most sea turtles reach sexual maturity at about age 50 and live another 30 years. Young readers may enjoy learning more about sea turtles by reading *Turtle Watch* by George Ancona and *Wonders of the Turtle World* by Wyatt Blassingame.

LESSON TO LEARN

Marlin and Nemo are Clown Fish and Dori is a Blue Tang. Both are only found in salt water.

TREASURE & TRIVIA

The character of Crush, the surf-talking sea turtle, was voiced by the director Andrew Stanton. It has been said that Andrew based the character after a cousin who lives in Long Beach, California; he mimicked the lingo and attitude.

Animation Academy—This is a 10 to 15 minute stage show in a smaller theater. The set is decked out like an artist's studio with crumpled paper, art books and Disney collectibles on the shelves. There are so many Mickeys hidden in plain sight that the challenge is seeing them all. A live animator teaches people how to draw some of Disney's most famous characters such as Mickey Mouse, Donald Duck, Goofy and Winnie the Pooh. The next few Hidden Mickeys listed aren't really hidden, but for anyone playing a scavenger hunt or seeking out hidden Mickeys with children, this attraction is the mother-lode.

HIDDEN MICKEY

On the right-hand side there is a deck of cards framed on the wall. Mickey Mouse is on the back of the cards.

HIDDEN MICKEY

Look for the Mickey Mouse watch wall hanging. It counts as a Hidden Mickey.

HIDDEN MICKEY

There are two large plush Mickeys.

HIDDEN MICKEY

On the upper shelves is an old toy that looks like a Rocking Horse only with a painted Mickey Mouse.

HIDDEN MICKEY

Beside the Rocking Horse is a drum set with Mickey's face. The shape of the drum also makes another Mickey silhouette.

HIDDEN MICKEY

By the stage door on the right-hand side is a tambourine with Mickey's face on it.

HIDDEN MICKEY

Also near the stage door on the right side is a plastic Mickey toy hanging on the wall.

HIDDEN MICKEY

Behind the animator's desk on the left side is a Mickey Mouse snow globe.

HIDDEN MICKEY

There is a set of book-ends on the bookshelf in the center of the stage that is a Mickey and a Minnie.

All of these Hidden Mickeys are real character merchandise sold throughout the years. Many of these toys are highly collectible.

Character Close Up—Now this area is used for a character meet and greet. Photographs and autographs from some of Disney's favorite characters can be obtained. As you walk around the queue notice the gallery that shows original art and character development from the first sketch to final art. Pulled from archives, these valuable sketches show some of Disney's most famous characters through the various stages of development. Be sure the kids have their autograph books and cameras ready.

Sorcerer's Workshop—The Sorcerer's Workshop has three interactive areas. The first room is the "Magic Mirror Realm," where there are bronze zoetropes and other early animation devices. Spin the wheels and look through the slits to see how the subtle changes in the drawing cause the characters to move. In just a few minutes you can create animation with the zoetropes.

On the tables you'll see long paper with pencils. Take your time and create a stick person doing cartwheels, or a bouncing ball or a kite waving in the wind or whatever you like. When you place the paper in the zoetropes, you can spin it and watch your drawings come to life.

TREASURE & TRIVIA

The zoetrope was invented in 1834 by William George Horner. It was an early form of motion picture projector that consisted of a drum, containing a set of still images that was turned in a circular fashion in order to create the illusion of motion. The zoetrope was named from the Greek root *Zoo* for "animal life" and *trope* for "things that turn."

LESSON TO LEARN

For all those people who are serious about becoming an animator, study the book *Illusion of Life* by Frank Thomas and Ollie Johnston. This book was written by two Disney legends who teach basic animation concepts such as squash and stretch and many other tips for making your own animation. Although hand-drawn animation is used very little today, computer animation uses the principals found in this book.

As you walk toward the back of the room you'll see crystal balls with animation in them. Notice how on one side you'll see a picture, and on the back side you'll see another picture that should coordinate with the first side. If you spin the card really fast you'll see how the eye is tricked into seeing the two images together.

Another way to create animation is to spin gold dials on the wall in the back room. Spin and look inside the tiny slits to see how the subtle changes in the drawing create movement.

TREASURE & TRIVIA

Look for hidden animated characters in the chandeliers. You might see Alice, Aladdin, Mulan and Simba.

HIDDEN MICKEY

There is another gold dial with a more difficult Hidden Mickey to spot. Find the gold dial with a treble clef and study the treble clef. The ears are off to the left side, but the head is part of this musical symbol.

Photo by Debbie Smith

HIDDEN MICKEY

Toward the back of the room on the left wall are gold dials that turn, causing the animation in the window to move. Look for a Hidden Mickey as a Sorcerer's Apprentice on the gold dial.

Photo by Debbie Smith

TREASURE & TRIVIA

Evil Queen's magic mirror has been moved from Snow White's former home and placed here in the Sorcerer's Workshop. Notice the Disney-fied zodiac around the mirror. Each sign has its "sun sign," or zodiac symbol, characterized by a Disney character. Can you find your sign?

Sign	Disney Character	Film
Taurus	Bulldog	*Lady and the Tramp*
Gemini	Tweedle Dee & Tweedle Dum	*Alice in Wonderland*
Cancer	Sebastian	*The Little Mermaid*
Leo	Simba	*The Lion King*
Virgo	Snow White	*Snow White & the Seven Dwarfs*
Libra	Lumiere	*Beauty and the Beast*
Scorpio	Flying Ship	*Atlantis*
Sagittarius	Robin Hood	*Robin Hood*
Capricorn	Djali	*Hunchback of Notre Dame*
Aquarius	King Triton	*The Little Mermaid*
Pisces	Cleo	*Pinocchio*
Aries	Phil	*Hercules*

TREASURE & TRIVIA

As you walk in the door, look to the left and behind you. You'll see a large Hidden Walt Disney. Although Walt Disney didn't invent animation, he did influence and improve the media significantly. Many people forget that Mickey Mouse was the first animated character who had a voice.

Beast's Library—Here you will read an interactive enchanted book. You'll hear the voices of Jerry Orbach (Lumiere) and David Ogden Stiers (Cogsworth) from the 1991 animated film *Beauty and the Beast*. Lumiere will ask you a series of questions to determine which Disney character you are most similar to. The original concept was to take guests pictures and morph the photo to

TREASURE & TRIVIA

Jerry Orbach was born in the Bronx October 20, 1935. Acting and singing was in his blood, as his father, Leon Orbach was a former vaudevillian. Disney fans recognize him as the voice of Lumiere from the 1991 animated film *Beauty and the Beast*. His character was so popular that he returned to record the voice for the direct-to-video sequels and the 2003 Magic Kingdom attraction, Mickey's Philharmagic. In 1995 he also voiced the character of Sa Ôluk in the direct-to-video film *Aladdin and the King of Thieves*. Jerry Orbach was a famous actor and singer aside from his Disney connection. He appeared in films, stage and television. In 1969 he won a Tony® for Best Actor in a Musical for *Promises, Promises*. He was nominated for a Tony® for Best Actor two other times, once for *Guys & Dolls* (1965) and again for *Chicago* (1976). During the 80s he worked on stage in *42ⁿᵈ Street*. In 1987 he played Dr. Jake Houseman in the film *Dirty Dancing*.

At the end of his life he played Detective Lennie Briscoe on the popular television show *Law & Order* (aired 1999 to 2005). He died of prostate cancer on December 28, 2004.

include the face and the Disney character. While the technology was available, the wait time and expense proved too much for the attraction.

While waiting for your turn in front of the enchanted book, notice how the entire room changes in relation to the magic rose over the fireplace. As the petals fall, the library becomes dark and sinister. Just as the last petal falls, Belle's voice is heard

LESSON TO LEARN

What's the difference between an Oscar, Tony, Grammy and an Emmy? All are the highest honors of their fields.

Oscar: Motion Picture (Film)
Tony: Theater
Grammy: Recording Industry (usually music)
Emmy: Television

TREASURE & TRIVIA

David Ogden Stiers was born October 31, 1942, in Peoria, IL, but was raised in Eugene, Oregon. He began his career at the Actor's Workshop in San Francisco and the California Shakespearean Theater in Santa Clara. He then went to New York and studied at Julliard. He is probably best known for his character Major Charles Emerson Winchester III from the hit television show M*A*S*H (1977 to 1983) and like his character, he is a devoted classical music fan and has conducted many orchestras. Disney fans recognize his long list of credits, including *Beauty and the Beast* (1991) where he voiced the character of Cogsworth, *Pocahontas* (1995) where he voiced the characters of Governor Ratcliffe and Wiggins, *The Hunchback of Notre Dame* (1996) where he voiced the Archdeacon, *Atlantis* (2001) where he voiced Fenton Q. Harcourt and *Lilo & Stitch* (2002) where he voiced Dr. Jumba Jookiba. He frequently returns to voice these characters in television shows, direct-to-DVD movies and even the popular Playstation2 game Kingdom Hearts II.

saying the ultimate magic words, "I love you," and the room is restored to its proper beauty. Miles of fiber optics transform the creepy den into a happy place as the Beast's curse is lifted.

TREASURE & TRIVIA

The Grand Slam of Show Business is to win an Oscar, Tony, Grammy and an Emmy. Only a few people have ever done it! The list includes Composer Richard Rodgers (of Rodgers and Hammerstein), Female Actor Helen Hayes, Female Actor Rita Moreno, Actor/Director John Gielgud, Female Actor Audrey Hepburn, Composer Marvin Hamlisch, Composer Jonathan Tunick, Actor/Writer/Producer/Director Mel Brooks and Producer/Director Mike Nichols.

HIDDEN MICKEY

The front of the fireplace makes a Hidden Mickey with a circle and some scroll work for the ears.

LESSON TO LEARN

Inspiration for the Beast's library in the film *Beauty and the Beast* must have been taken from the British Museum in London. For all those book worms, it is exciting to learn that the library really exists.

TREASURE & TRIVIA

Beauty and the Beast was the first animated film to be nominated for an Oscar for Best Picture by Academy of Motion Picture Arts and Sciences. The Academy nominated the film for seven categories and it won "Best Song" for "Beauty and the Beast" and "Best Score" both written by Howard Ashman and Alan Menken. Angela Lansbury returned to Disney to play Mrs. Potts and sing the title song. Her first Disney film was *Bedknobs and Broomsticks* released in 1971.

Ursula's Grotto—In the underwater caverns, you supply the voices for difference characters from famous Disney films. First you choose to act or sing. If you choose to act you may choose between *Bambi, Aladdin, Lion King* or *Beauty and the Beast.* If you choose to sing, your scene choices are "Unbirthday Song," "Heigh Ho," "The Bare Necessities" or "Hakuna Matata." After a rehearsal, you record your lines. Then the film clip is played back using your voice. The experience is sure to give you a laugh.

TREASURE & TRIVIA

Hans Christian Andersen's story of a little mermaid was a concept that Walt Disney was playing with during his lifetime. In November 1989 *The Little Mermaid* was released in theaters, renewing the era of animation. It won Academy Awards for Best Song with "Under the Sea" and also Best Score. The film was particularly tricky because all the under water scenes needed constant motion, bubbles and ripples.

TREASURE & TRIVIA

Pat Carroll gives Ursula her voice and Jodi Benson gives Ariel her voice. You'll hear both in Ursula's Grotto introduction sequence.

Off the Page Retail Shop: Notice the Dumbo outline on the side walk. He has literally flown off the page and is on the marquis at the entrance of the store.

Photo by Debbie Smith

Dumbo has literally flown "off the page" giving the store inspiration for its name.

Famous California architecture dresses the Hollywood Pictures Backlot.

Restrooms—It may seem strange to make the restrooms note-worthy, but outside of the Animation Building the restrooms are hidden behind a magnificent façade. The entry uses the architectural style of Frank Lloyd Wright and the homes he designed in Los Angeles in 1923. Using decorated concrete blocks, the block style is similar to the Storer House, but the design with the windows and roof-line looks more like the Freeman House. To read more about the famous architect Frank Lloyd Wright, look in The Grand Californian Hotel chapter.

PlayHouse Disney— Live on Stage!

Based on the Disney channel show, Bear Tutter, Pip and Pop are there to entertain. Rolie Polie Olie,

Stanley and other Disney Channel favorites appear and entertain the youngsters. This show is great for toddlers, as they will recognize the characters.

Parents should be warned that there are very few benches inside the Playhouse Disney show. Most everyone sits on the floor and kids are encouraged to stand up to sing and dance during the show.

The building façade is an Art Deco replica inspired by the ABC Radio Building on Vine Street in Hollywood. On opening day the building housed the Soap Opera Bistro. Many ABC soap opera stars were on hand to dedicate the restaurant and each soap opera star left a television prop from their show. The television show *Port Charles* left tarot cards and a crystal ball, *All My Children* left a flask, *One Life to Live* left the commissioner's badge and *General Hospital* left Luke and Laura's wedding rings. In fact, actor Robert Woods from *One Life to Live* mentioned that he was at Disneyland on public opening day July 18, 1955, and later became a cast member working on the Pirates of the Caribbean attraction. Each room of the restaurant was designed to look like a television set from one of the ABC soaps. The servers dressed up in costumes and would ad lib according to their character for the day. Sadly, the restaurant didn't stay busy enough to keep it open.

The buildings hiding the attractions are given soundstage numbers to blend in with the idea of being on a movie lot. Ironically, The Walt Disney Studios in Burbank has only four soundstages. Dave Smith of Disney Archives shared that the Disney Studios had only two soundstages during Walt's lifetime. The soundstages or buildings with soundstage numbers at Hollywood Pictures Backlot are fictional and not even chronological. It is unknown if the numbers represent anything.

DCA Sound Stages
12 (Hollywood & Dine)
15 PlayHouse Disney
16 Monsters Inc.
17 Millionaire (formerly)
21 Hyperion Theater
23 Muppets Vision 3D

Playhouse Disney to the right and the trompe l'oeil in the center. Trompe l'oeil is a prominent feature in Hollywood Pictures Backlot.

Grizzly River Peak is a park icon and tribute to the California Grizzly on the

Chapter 4

Golden State

The Golden State area is the most diverse of the themed lands. It has five separate themed areas within it and it creates a large circle in the middle of the Park with Grizzly River Peak in the center. Usually guests experience half of the Golden State area, for example seeing Condor Flats, Grizzly Peak Recreation Area and the Bay Area and moving on to Paradise Pier. Later, you may come around the opposite direction and re-enter the Golden State land by seeing the Pacific Wharf and Golden Winery. Since the area is so varied and has so many themes, it doesn't really spoil the experience to exit and re-enter the land. Instead, it might make you appreciate the diverse topography of California.

Condor Flats:

This area of Golden State is inspired by the rich 1930s aviation history in California. The area in Condor Flats around the hangar suggests the Vandenberg Air Force Base with a dusty landscape re-creating a high-

desert airfield. Many famous people such as Howard Hughes, Amelia Earhart, Charles Lindbergh, Chuck Yeager and others have ties to California, as you'll see in the Soarin' queue and can read about further in the appendix of this book. Yet, it was the hard work of many not-so-famous Californians to build the aircraft that made these

All the areas of Golden State are listed on this sign.

pilots renowned. You'll also find the celebrated planes in the appendix with a paragraph about each plane's contribution to the development of aviation.

TREASURE & TRIVIA

On the outside of the Quonset hut that is the Taste Pilots' Grill Restaurant, look at the plane crashing out the front. This is an orange replica of Bell X-1, the plane that Capt. Charles "Chuck" Yeager flew to break the sound barrier on October 14, 1947. He reached a speed of 670 mph at an altitude of 42,000 feet. The plane was nicknamed "Glamorous Glennis" after Yeager's wife. The actual Bell X-1 plane is on permanent display at the Smithsonian National Air and Space Museum in Washington, D.C.

TREASURE & TRIVIA

Where do we get the term Quonset hut? During World War II, the Navy needed a way to quickly provide shelter for people and materials. The Navy hired George A. Fuller Construction Company to build a cheap, lightweight and portable building. Two men, Peter Dejongh and Otto Brandenberger, went to work setting up near Quonset, Rhode Island. Within a month, the Quonset hut was in production, even while the design still required tinkering.

TREASURE & TRIVIA

Fly 'n' Buy has a calendar near the register with the date October 14, 1947, circled. This day is significant because it is the day that Chuck Yeager flew the Bell X-1 faster than the speed of sound and was the first person to do so. The broken clock above the calendar shows the exact time he did it.

Photo by Debbie Smith

HIDDEN MICKEY

Go inside the Taste Pilots' Grill and look for the fire alarms on the back wall of the restaurant. On the right side, you'll see high near the ceiling a Hidden Mickey made from the alarm bells.

HIDDEN MICKEY

Once you find the fire alarms that look like a Hidden Mickey, look at the engine photos below it. The photo is hard to discern, but the Hidden Mickey is not. The Hidden Mickey is made up of part of an engine.

OPENING DAY ATTRACTION

Soarin' Over California

One of the most innovative attractions created by the Walt Disney Company is *Soarin' Over California*. What's particularly great about Soarin' is that it appeals to many ages. An elderly person can ride it without fear of being thrown around too much, yet young people enjoy the whole effect. You are gently hoisted 50 feet in the air, placed in the middle of an 80-foot curved movie screen and feel as though you are hang gliding. "A flat screen didn't give us the realism we wanted . . . " said the Executive Show Director Rick Rothschild. The

The monorail glides in front of Soarin' Over California.

screen is domed and wraps 180 degrees around you to improve the effect, while smells and sound recreate a five-minute flight. There are two screens in the building and each show can accommodate 87 people per room, making capacity near 1,491 per hour.

Mark Sumner created the original ride system over Thanksgiving holiday in 1996 when he sketched out the mechanism, but realized it would be very difficult to explain. So he pulled out his 1950s era erector set and built a working model, where you could turn the crank and the three seats would gently lift into the air. The Imagineering team was a little nervous that the mechanism would work safely on a larger scale. Some engineering research demonstrated that it would be possible. Mark is quoted in "Tales of the Laughing Place" as saying, "The mechanism that's out there is exactly like the model I built. We get from the high tech, the latest virtual reality technology, to the low tech, which is a 1950s kid's toy." Constructed with more than a million pounds of steel, the mechanism can gently lift more than 37 tons. The ride vehicle also tilts and pivots to enhance the viewing experience. Once in the "cruising altitude," the seats move approximately 30 inches and tilt back and forth approximately 5 degrees in each direction.

The next hurdle was creating the film. Usually films are shot at 24 frames per second, but with an oversized screen, so few frames can create a strobing effect. Instead, Imagineers used an increased speed of 48 frames per second to prevent the strobing, but that created projection issues. According to Alec Scribner, "The increased speed of the film moving through the projector meant that WDI had to specifically tailor the patented Omni-max projectors to cope with the increased demand on their moving parts."

Lastly, filming would create its own set of challenges. In the same article from "Tales of the Laughing Place," director Rick Rothschild said, "Airspace within U.S. National Parks is restricted and you have to have a permit. A helicopter had not been allowed to fly within Yosemite National Park since the middle of last century, when

Chuck Yeager is just one of the aviation greats honored in the Soarin' queue.

the Park was closed to visitors due to a flood! Eventually we were able to secure the permit, but it only provided for a four-hour window. We would have to shoot within that period even if the weather was awful. Thankfully, it was a beautiful day! Even the Point Lobos sequence was tough to film, as it is a protected marine sanctuary. It took a year to get all the necessary permits."

As you queue in the hangar the first two rooms are a gallery of California's famous pilots and planes. The wait never seems long enough here because there is so much to read and learn. If this information is of particular interest to you, go to the appendix to learn more.

The pre-board film is narrated by "Patrick, your chief flight attendant." The actor is Patrick Warburton, who is most famous for his role as David Puddy on *Seinfeld.* He has voiced characters for Disney, including Kronk in *The Emperor's New Groove*, Mr. Barkin in *Kim Possible* and Patrick in *Home on the Range.*

HIDDEN MICKEY

The kid needing the safety strap is wearing Mickey sweats with a Grumpy shirt. Don't forget to count the Mousketeer hat worn by the older man.

Ever want to visit the cities and Parks Soarin' flies over? The pre-board film tells you roughly where the scenes were filmed. Californians may recognize these areas, but just in case a couple stump you, here is the list in the order shown in the film.

- San Francisco
- Redwood Creek
- Napa Valley
- Monterey Bay
- Lake Tahoe
- Yosemite
- Palm Springs
- Camarillo
- Anza-Borrego
- San Diego
- Malibu
- Los Angeles
- Disneyland

TREASURE & TRIVIA

In the pre-board film, keep a sharp eye out for the last two passengers in the front row. They are wearing early 20th century flight gear.

HIDDEN MICKEY

The film has several Hidden Mickeys and fun things to keep a sharp eye out for. The first one is the hardest to spot. As the golf ball flies right at you in the Palm Springs sequence of the movie, look for the Hidden Mickey painted on the ball.

HIDDEN MICKEY

As the film flies over Disneyland, keep a sharp eye out for three more Mickeys.

1) The Mickey flowers at the entrance plaza
2) Mickey and Minnie are in the Christmas Parade skating on a float wearing blue holiday outfits
3) Finally in the third burst of fireworks, three explosions make up the famous icon shape. Tinker Bell will try to distract you, that's why the fireworks Mickey is considered a Hidden Mickey.

Here is a replica of the Glamourous Glennis, Chuck Yeager's plane that was the first to break the sound barrier.

TREASURE & TRIVIA

In the Condor Flats area you might see a few Space Shuttle main engine nozzles. Most popular is the one that sprays guests with water mist in front of the Soarin' queue. These Space Shuttle nozzles are designed and built in Southern California by Boeing. The Space Shuttle requires three of them to provide propulsion to boost the shuttle into orbit. The nozzles together provide the equivalent of 37 million horsepower, as compared to a car, which usually has 100 to 200 horsepower.

Following the curve of the walkway, you'll leave Condor Flats and discover the next area of the Golden State: Grizzly Peak Recreation Area. The transition is subtle as an older plane is on display, then a billboard with the Grizzly rock and eventually hiking signs. The pavement changes, the desert landscape changes to a green, forest-like area and in a matter of a few steps, you've traveled hundreds of miles in California.

Grizzly Peak Recreation Area

The icon symbol for DCA is Grizzly Peak, a 110-foot-high, faux granite mountain. The summit of the mountain is the shape of a growling California grizzly bear. This area of the Golden State represents the wilds of Sequoia and Yosemite National Parks and the wilderness of northern California. This mini-wilderness is developed in only eight small acres, although it feels like a lot more, thanks in great part to the landscape of pine trees, natural grasses and sequoias.

OPENING DAY ATTRACTION

Grizzly River Run

This ride is known as the "wettest wildest white wateriest raft ride southwest of the Sierra." Amid gold mine ruins, passengers board their circular raft and are pulled up a 275-foot conveyor belt to begin

It's hard to imagine that Grizzly Peak grew from the former parking lot of Disneyland.

The Grizzly bear suited up for rafting is reminiscent of the road signs in Northern California. Inspired by the signs of Paul Bunyan and Babe the Blue ox.

packages and backpacks while you ride Grizzly River Run (GRR).

The journey lasts about five-and-a-half minutes, carrying eight riders per raft. In an hour, about 2,067 people go through GRR. The raft ascends 45 feet and floats downhill from there. Fast-moving currents send adventurers spinning and splashing, bouncing off boulders and floating through an erupting geyser field. There are two major drops, Bear Claw Falls, which is about 10 feet, and Wash Out Falls, which is 22 feet with a 30 degree angle. It's Wash Out Falls that earns GRR the distinction of being the world's tallest, fastest river ride.

their white water thrill. You'll travel past a dilapidated wheelhouse, plunge through a cavern, getting a good look at Grizzly Peak, travel through a mineshaft and through a field of geysers. You are pretty much guaranteed to get wet.

TIP: This attraction is known for "the wetter, the better." You will get wet—very wet. Unless you have a change of clothes, it's best to buy a rain poncho at the store next door. You'll still get a little wet with the poncho, but you won't be soaked completely through, which can be uncomfortable later in the day. The ponchos are less than $10 and fold up nicely in your bag. There is also a free locker rental for your

A fun way to cool down on a hot summer day.

A rock outside the entrance to GRR tells
the Indian Legend of the mountain.

The Myth

Long ago a coyote named "ah hale met oo soo" met a grizzly bear. The coyote asked the grizzly to watch over and protect the lands, and the grizzly bear agreed. Soon, people came and tried to chase away the grizzly, but he stood fast. When the coyote returned, over 50 men came to chase away the grizzly, but the grizzly would not leave, so the coyote turned the grizzly to stone so that he could watch over the land for all time. It is believed that you can hear his spirit at the summit.

Many years later, gold miners came to pan Grizzly Peak. Miners would scatter over the mountain and pan for gold. Eventually the mountain dried up and no gold has been found there for years. Many miners abandoned their equipment with the hope that they'd return someday and find their riches.

Instead, Grizzly Peak offers a new breed of riches to rafters known as "White Water River Rats." River Rats discovered the thrilling experience of "tubing down the river." The Grizzly Peak Rafting Company has set up shop and enables visitors to enjoy the wilds of Grizzly River up close. However, as you enter the cave directly under the bear, you may hear him growl.

Photo by Debbie Smith

There are signs and markings all over the mountain. If you weren't traveling so fast you might get the chance to enjoy some of the funny stories they tell.

Authentic gold mining and crushing equipment is found in the queue of Grizzly River Run.

Photo by Debbie Smith

TREASURE & TRIVIA

Look at the abandoned equipment near the GRR loading area. The rusty ore crushers are from the Gold Rush era. They were found in the Sierra Nevadas by Imagineer Chris Tietz.

TREASURE & TRIVIA

As you're riding Grizzly River Run and finish your ascent to the top of the hill, keep a sharp eye out for a sign with the elevation of 1,401. This is not the elevation of Grizzly Mountain, but instead the street number for the Imagineering building in Glendale.

Rushin' River Store is a pun on the Russian River in California, 25 miles west of Santa Rosa and 10 miles east of the Pacific Ocean. The town features wonderful outdoor activities, such as hiking, fishing, camping and wine tasting. Ironically, "rushin'" isn't really a good word to describe the Russian River as the waters are calm and slow moving, great for canoeing.

LESSON TO LEARN

The California Grizzly, like the one the mountain resembles, is the California state mammal and is represented on the state flag and seal.

TREASURE & TRIVIA

The building is named Eureka Gold and Timber Company. Eureka is Greek for "I have found it" and was a popular exclamation among the miners when they found gold. Eureka is also the name of a city in northern California on the coast. The discovery of gold at Sutter's Mill in 1848 spawned the rush of prospectors to California.

Photo by Debbie Smith

TREASURE & TRIVIA

There is a plaque giving tribute to the Pelton wheel as you exit the Grizzly Peak Recreation area. The wheel on the wheelhouse is a Pelton wheel, which is one of the most efficient types of water wheels. It was invented around 1876 to 1879 by Lester Allan Pelton while he was working in California. Notice the spoon-shaped buckets on the edge of the wheel. The weight of the water in the bucket reverses the flow of water, causing the turbine to spin. Two pairs of buckets are mounted on the wheel to keep balance and smooth momentum.

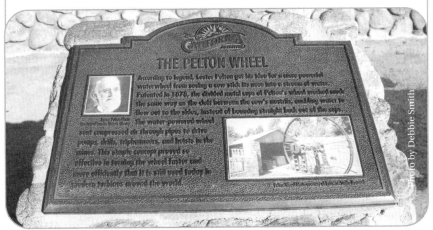

Photo by Debbie Smith

The Redwood trees are famous for being so large you can drive a car through them.

OPENING DAY ATTRACTION

Redwood Creek Challenge Trail

Here kids can explore a cavern, climb inside a hollow tree, climb over rocks, bounce on rope bridges, scale cargo nets and track animals found in California. Kids can learn the different markings and follow quail, mountain lion and elk tracks. Similar to the National Parks, there are ranger station towers in Redwood Creek Challenge Trail. Climb the log towers for an excellent view. One tower provides brave kids the chance to glide down 60-foot-long zip lines.

TREASURE & TRIVIA

Brother Bear is a full-length Disney animated film released in 2003. *Brother Bear* was the last film to be produced in the Disney's-MGM Studio before it closed. Directed by Aaron Blaise and Robert Walker, the film features music by Phil Collins and the voices of Joaquin Phoenix as Kenai and Jeremy Suarez as Koda. The two moose add a lot of humor to the film, voiced by Rick Moranis as Rutt and Dave Thomas as Tuke. The plot is about three brothers. When a bear is blamed for taking the life of the oldest brother, the youngest brother, Kenai, kills the bear in revenge. Magically, Kenai is transformed into a bear himself, only to be hunted by his middle brother. The only way for Kenai to survive is to befriend a grizzly cub named Koda who shows him the true meaning of brotherhood.

Brother Bear totem pole greets guests near the entrance to Redwood Creek Challenge Trail.

HIDDEN MICKEY

There are three Hidden Mickeys on the map at the entrance to Redwood Creek Challenge Trail. Look mostly to the left side of the map, and disregard the traditional black color and look for the three circle shapes.

There are three Hidden Mickeys on this sign, but you'll need to see it in person to find them.

Photo by Debbie Smith

LESSON TO LEARN

The Ahwahnee Hotel is the luxurious four-star hotel built in Yosemite Park. It opened in 1927 in the midst of the Sierra Mountains and is designated as a National Historic Landmark. You might see a glimpse of it in the *Soarin' Over California* film at the base of Half Dome.

Ahwahnee Camp Circle has storytellers recite Native American tribal stories by day and ghost stories by night. Characters Kenai and Koda from the Disney animated film

Brother Bear meet for photos. Many of the other wood-carved creatures are the subjects of the stories told at the Ahwahnee Camp Circle.

Photo by Debbie Smith

HIDDEN MICKEY

In one tower, there is a radio with the aviation letters spelled out, A= alpha, B= beta, C= Charlie, but the M, which should be "Mike," is Mickey instead.

LESSON TO LEARN

According to the website www.yosemite.ca.us, Ahwahnee originally referred to the largest and most powerful Indian village in the Yosemite Valley. The Native American people who lived there called themselves Ah-wah-ne-chee or "dwellers of Ahwahnee."

A small replica of the Palace of Fine Arts rotunda in San Francisco.

The Bay Area

Imagineers tried to create the "City by the Bay" with a little of the San Francisco architecture. The architecture is inspired by the Victorian homes and Presidio Park. A replica of the San Francisco Palace of Fine Arts sits next to Paradise Bay with a 45-foot-tall rotunda.

Unlike Disneyland, where the second-floor windows are dedications and theme park credits, Disney's California Adventure took a different spin. The windows in the Bay Area are puns, rhymes and jokes referring to sights, cities and references in different regions of the state.

- Fisherman's Dwarf is posted rather than Fisherman's Wharf
- Presidio Video Post Production
- Sausalito Maritime Bank, Floating Loans since 1898
- Island Cell Phones Alcatraz Prop

- Cable Car Financial – Riding the ups and downs of finances
- Beat Publishing Poetry Novels
- Lock Alcatraz
- Palo Alto Saxophones High notes/low prices
- Knob Hill Door, hardware and locks
- Gold and State Attorneys at Law

TREASURE & TRIVIA

Notice the address numbers of the buildings on one side of the street. The numbers double: 16, 32, 64, 128, 256 and 512. The computer savvy may recognize the proximity of the Silicon Valley to San Francisco and that these numbers represent the number of bits handled by a particular processor. In the early computer days, there were 16-bit and then the memory doubled and then doubled again. If you buy a disk or a memory stick, the increments are 16, 32, 64, 128, etc.

OPENING DAY ATTRACTION

Golden Dreams

When you're ready for a short break, catch the 22-minute film featuring the history and people of California. Hosted by Califia, the spirit of California, you journey into the history of the generations of immigrants that were drawn to

Outside the Golden Dreams theater is a 14-by-100-foot mural that depicts 500 years of California history.

California. Introducing you to the Chumash Indians, Spanish missionaries, the miners of 1849, Chinese railroad builders, farmers, Hollywood moguls, 1960s flower children and more recently the Silicon Valley entrepreneurs, you get a sense of diversity of the California people. The film was directed by award-winning director Agnieszka Holland and shot in 16 locations representing 16 points in the state's history. The theater has 350 seats decorated in the Art Deco style and can accommodate about 1,050 people per hour.

Heather Headley sings the touching music for the show, written by Walter Afanasieff with lyrics by John Bettis. The montage of famous Californians at the end of the film is very popular. Look for some famous faces, such as Ronald Reagan and Richard Nixon, former U.S. presidents from California; Walt Disney at the Rose Parade a little less than a year before he died; and Chuck Yeager with Glamourous Glennis. The short clip with Habitat for Humanity shows Disneyland cast members volunteering their time.

TREASURE & TRIVIA

The movie features Whoopi Goldberg as the fabled goddess Califia. You might even recognize Whoopi's face in the pillars on both sides of the stage.

LESSON TO LEARN

The name for California comes from a Spanish romance book published in 1510. It was about an island paradise near the Indies where the beautiful goddess Califia ruled over a country of beautiful black Amazons with lots of pearls and gold. Men were only allowed there one day a year to help perpetuate the race. Cortez' men thought they found the island in 1535 because they found pearls.

LESSON TO LEARN

In the *Golden Dreams* film, during the story segment, a lot of real people are referenced. See if you can catch them and perhaps be inspired to read more about:

- William "Bill" Mulholland (engineer)
- John Muir (conservationist)
- Dorothea Lange (photographer)
- Louis B. Mayer (head of MGM movie studio)
- Adrian Adolph Greenberg (costume designer)
- César Chávez (farm worker/ labor leader/activist)
- Steve Jobs and Steven Wozniak (co-founders of Apple Computer)

Pacific Wharf

The wood and brick waterfront buildings were inspired by Monterey's Cannery Row. The street was once a series of fish processing plants but now has retail businesses and restaurants.

LESSON TO LEARN

A book was written about Cannery Row in 1945 by John Steinbeck. In 1958, Ocean View Avenue in Monterey, Calif. changed its name to Cannery Row in honor of the book. You'll see the book and famous town are referenced in the windows alongside the Boudin Bakery.

The window is a tribute to Monterey, California; the town made famous by Steinbeck's book.

Photo by Debbie Smith

LESSON TO LEARN

John Steinbeck is a renowned American novelist, playwright and storyteller. He was a native Californian born in Salinas on February 27, 1902. He studied marine biology at Stanford University but never finished his degree, because he knew he wanted to be a writer. His first book was *Cup of Gold* written in 1929, which didn't get much recognition. He continued to write such classics as *Tortilla Flat* (1935), *Of Mice and Men* (1937), *The Grapes of Wrath* (1939), *Cannery Row* (1945), *The Pearl* (1947), *East of Eden* (1952), *The Winter of Our Discontent* (1961) and many more. Steinbeck often created his stories around people who are struggling and underprivileged. Hollywood loves Steinbeck and made films of several of his novels and continues to do so, such as rumors of Ron Howard's 2009 version of *East of Eden*. In the 1940s, John Steinbeck moved to New York and traveled abroad as an internationally famous writer. It is believed he longed for California and even wrote *Cannery Row* while in New York. In 1945, Steinbeck was nominated for an Academy Award for his work on Alfred Hitchcock's film *Lifeboat*. In 1962, he won the Nobel Prize for Literature for *The Grapes of Wrath*. On December 20, 1968, John Steinbeck passed away of heart disease in Sag Harbor, New York.

BRIAN McKIM

Mission Tortilla Factory

hosted by Mission Foods: ODA
Tour the micro-factory and watch
how corn and flour tortillas are
made. Taste one fresh off the
machine and learn recipes on how
to prepare popular meals using tortillas. Sometimes the tortilla factory
gives out recipes and edible Disney
tortilla decals. If it's your birthday,
they often celebrate by giving you a
bag of tortillas.

TREASURE & TRIVIA

L os Angeles has more people of
Mexican ancestry than any
other urban area in the world
outside of Mexico.

The Boudin Bakery

hosted by Boudin Bakery
Tour this micro-factory and watch
a short video with Rosie O'Donnell
and Colin Mochrie. They share with
you a history of sourdough bread
and the Boudin family bakery. In
the bakery you can see the loaves of
bread in the many phases of prepa-
ration. The Boudins' secret family
recipe dates back to 1850.

Once you're finished with the
micro-factory tours, you may want
to grab a bite. You'll have a choice
of Cocina Cucamonga Mexican
Grill or the Pacific Wharf Café,
where Boudin's bread bowls are a
big hit. Something interesting
about this area that you won't find
at Disneyland is the beer bar and
the margarita stand. Guests must
be at least 21 years old to purchase
alcohol.

TREASURE & TRIVIA

B oth Los Angeles and San
Francisco claim to have
invented the fortune cookie,
not China.

HIDDEN MICKEY

Sourdough bread in the
shape of a Mickey Mouse is a
Hidden Mickey you can purchase and take home with you.

Photo by Debbie Smith

TREASURE & TRIVIA

Chinese dragons hanging from the rafters stretch up to 100 feet long from nose to tail. One is named Derrick the Dude with bright blue and green satin scales, while Darion, his fire-breathing sister, has a glittery purple and red hide. Inspired by traditional Chinese parade kits, they were made by Flying Colors out of Berkeley.

Darion is the name of the female dragon.

OPENING DAY ATTRACTION

Golden Vine Winery

Here in DCA, the Imagineers tried to create a mini Napa Valley with the scenery changing from rustic in the back to agriculture in the vineyard. There are 350 grapevines growing near the mission-style house. This area is both a micro-vineyard and a wine-tasting facility. Imagineers provide plaques to help you identify and pronounce the different grape varietals. There is also a plaque that helps you identify the different growing seasons of the vines.

Keep in mind that although grapes come in both red and white,

Photo by Debbie Smith

Golden Vine Winery was originally sponsored by Robert Mondavi, and the mission-style house still represents his influence.

the juice is always clear. Red wine is made when the skins are pulped with the juice. Down one of the paths, you may see two plaques that describe the types of grapes that are used to make both red and white wines.

Plaque with Red: Merlot, Cabernet Sauvignon, Pinot Noir, Syrah and Zinfandel.

Plaque with White: Moscato Bianco, Chardonnay, Riesling, Sauvignon Blanc and Pinot Grigio.

California is known for producing excellent wines. Napa Valley is known for Cabernet Sauvignon, although they grow all varietals. Sonoma Valley is known for Chardonnay and Pinot Noir and south central coast is known for all varietals.

TREASURE & TRIVIA

Back in 1884, Anaheim was a rich farmland. The main crop was surprisingly not oranges, but grapes. Orange County produced more than a million gallons of wine back in the day. Pierce's Disease ruined the crops, and the farmers switched to growing oranges. Later, Orange County would be given its name, derived from its most plentiful crop.

Golden Vine Winery is popular because wine tasting is available for adults. Originally, the wine tasting was sponsored by Robert Mondavi Winery, but now it represents several vintners. Typically there are three wine-tasting programs, each with a variety of wines to try. Each season the programs change and

Photo by Debbie Smith

offer the repeat customer a new series. The cast members are very knowledgeable and will share with you some basic fundamentals about what to look at, smell and taste. One of the fascinating things about wine is you may develop your palate to identify different flavors, such as vanilla, berries, citrus, coffee bean, oak or hundreds of other flavors.

Seasons of the Vine

This show is about seven-and-a-half minutes long and is set in a 50-seat wine aging room. Narrated by Jeremy Irons, the show explains the process of wine-making. The film describes the vineyard seasons, revealing the complex and delicate process. The smell of aged wine fills the air. Some famous winemakers appear in the film, including Heather Pyle, using the refractometer. The man with the beard is Ken Brown. You may also spot Robert Mondavi with his two sons Tim and Michael.

 LESSON TO LEARN

What is a refractometer? It measures the approximate value of potential degree of alcohol in the grape before it is fermented.

 **LESSON TO LEARN**

Heather Pyle is an instructor at San Joaquin Delta College and a wine-making consultant. She is relatively famous in California wine circles.

 **LESSON TO LEARN**

Ken Brown of Ken Brown Wines in Santa Barbara County specializes in Pinot Noir. He has spent over 20 years in winemaking to understand the elusive traits that make a great Pinot Noir.

 **LESSON TO LEARN**

Although the Disney staff is always gracious and would never allow a guest to feel embarrassed, the first lesson in wine education is never, ever order White Zinfandel. Zinfandel is a red wine. While in wine country a friend was warned not to order White Zin and when he did, he was denied service and asked to leave. So as the wine-dyed T-shirt says, "Friends don't let friends drink White Zin."

LESSON TO LEARN

Robert Mondavi was born June 18, 1913, in Virginia, Minn. He is the son of wine makers from Italy. He graduated from Stanford in 1937 and made his career as a successful vineyard operator by making technical improvements and marketing. He gave recognition to Napa Valley. In 1965, he opened his own winery in Oakville (located in Napa Valley) after working in the family business. In 1968, he made a dry, oak-aged Sauvignon Blanc, an unpopular varietal at the time, and labeled it "Fume Blanc." The wine proved to be very successful and is synonymous with Sauvignon Blanc. During his career, he has developed a number of premium wines and earned the respect of connoisseurs and vintners. In 1979, he acquired Woodbridge Winery in Lodi, Calif. In 1997, the Grand European Jury Wine Tasting Reserve had a blind taste testing and a Robert Mondavi Chardonnay was ranked first place. In 2004, Constellation Brands bought the Robert Mondavi winery for $1.36 billion. The corporation now has wineries around the world. In Davis, Calif., there is a performing arts center named the Mondavi Center on his behalf. To read more about Robert Mondavi, buy his autobiography, *Harvest of Joy: How the Good Life became Great Business* (1998).

LESSON TO LEARN

The Court of Masters has schooling and honors that it bestows on its students. A dedicated student of wine who passes the first two-day written and tasting exam is called a level 1 sommelier. Disneyland has a training program that educates their food and beverage staff using the Court of Masters program. Each year, Disney celebrates the addition of approximately 15 to 20 new level 1 sommeliers. Look for a small red pin next to the cast member's name tag so that you may get the best recommendations. The classes are taught by a level 3 sommelier Michael Jordan. There are four levels of sommelier, and each step is believed to be 10 times harder than the previous. There are only 47 master sommeliers in the United States and 104 in the world.

Golden Vine Winery

Pixar characters inspired the "a bug's land" area. The character Gypsy Moth was

a bug's land

To get to a bug's land you have to cross through the Bountiful Valley Farm area. The gardens start to prepare you for fun as the planters are themed with characters. Bountiful Valley Farm was formerly sponsored by Caterpillar, and the kids loved to climb on the farming equipment. In Disney fashion, some edutainment takes place as California is recognized for its significant contribution to the world's food supply.

Bountiful Valley Farm –
presented by Caterpillar

While the theme remains agricultural, the valley is no longer Napa, but Imperial instead. The Imperial Valley is a world-renowned region for growing produce. California is the number one producer of more than 350 crops. For the gardener in the group, the area is filled with native California crops, such as avocados, artichokes, citrus fruits and more. All of these foods are grown and harvested onsite.

Kids love to climb on the Caterpillar vehicles in Bountiful Valley Farm.

Toward the back of the area are two displays where Flik may greet guests. Focusing on the significance of California farming, one display is called "Outstanding in their field." The display is ever-changing and highlights successful farmers and ranchers. Another display shows that although California can grow many different types of fruits and vegetables, not all of them survive this climate. "Crops that flopped" shows what few products can't grow in California.

The gardens in this area are wonderful. The *Bug's Life* characters catch your attention, but the flowers and landscaping are really very interesting. It's a nice quiet place to stroll away from the crowds and appreciate the work of the Disney gardening team, assisted by the Pixar characters. In both the *It's Tough to be a Bug!*® show and also in Flik's "Fun" Fair, you'll get the impression that you've been miniaturized to see the world from a bug's perspective. The transition begins to take place in Bountiful Valley Farm.

Farmers Expo is where guests can learn about California's agriculture.

Photo by Debbie Smith

FARMERS EXPO

A little stage is set up with some exhibits that talk about the importance of agriculture to California's economy. Here, some guests can learn more about fruit, vegetables, wine and the ranching industries. This is a wonderful tribute to the farming and ranching communities

Rosie, voiced by Bonnie Hunt.

Heimlich, voiced by Joe Ranft.

Francis, voiced by Denis Leary.

Slim, voiced by David Hyde Pierce.

Photo by Debbie Smith

The Farmers Expo stage is a nice place to rest and sometimes catch some live entertainment.

in California. It's interesting to read about the significant contributions Californians have made in the agriculture industry.

TREASURE & TRIVIA

David Jacks is credited as the first person to have marketed Monterey Jack Cheese in Monterey, Calif., in the late 1880s. For the Disney trivia buffs, Monterey Jack was also the name of a character on the Disney Afternoon television lineup from a show called *Rescue Rangers* starring Chip and Dale.

TREASURE & TRIVIA

There are 1.74 million dairy cows in California producing milk, making California the number one dairy state. (But don't tell New Jersey.)

TREASURE & TRIVIA

California cows produce six to seven gallons of milk daily. It takes 10 to 12 pounds of milk to make one pound of cheese, although it is probable that if you ate one pound of cheese you might gain some of that 10 to 12 pounds back!

TREASURE & TRIVIA

More than half of the world's raisin supply is grown in California, and most of the raisins are grown within 50 miles of Fresno.

In 1923, Anaheim horticulturist Rudolph Boysen crossed the raspberry, blackberry and loganberry and created the boysenberry.

Olive trees have great longevity. In 1770, Spanish missions planted olive trees that still produce olives today.

In 1893, the U.S. Supreme Court rendered an opinion that tomatoes are vegetables. Actually, they were wrong; tomatoes are fruit.

According to www.greatvalley.org, California produces 99% of the United States almonds, artichokes, dates, figs, kiwifruit, olives, prunes, raisins, persimmons, pistachios and walnuts.

In 1881, Judge James Harvey Logan of Santa Cruz introduced the loganberry by crossing a red raspberry and a California wild blackberry.

The first Hass avocado tree was grown in the late 1920s by Rudolph Hass, who discovered a certain strain of avocado in his La Habra backyard and named it the Hass avocado. Hass patented it in 1935. La Habra is less than 10 miles north of the Disneyland Resort.

California is the number two grower of cotton, and cotton is California's number one agricultural export commodity.

Did you know that carrots come in orange, yellow and purple?

In the 1860s an English settler named William Thompson planted Mediterranean grapes north of Sacramento. Today, we call those Thompson Seedless grapes.

California is the only successful growing area in the United States for pistachios, which require a warm, temperate zone.

TREASURE & TRIVIA

California grows approximately 80% of the world's almonds, due to its perfect climate.

Honey bees are the only insect that produce a food eaten by humans.

TREASURE & TRIVIA

Note the early change already. In just a few short years, this area changed its name from Bountiful Valley Farm to a bug's land.

Irrigation Station

This is an area with pipes spraying water to cool guests down. It is a simple maze of sprinklers and water gates that open and close when triggered.

OPENING DAY ATTRACTION

It's Tough to be a Bug!®

This eight-and-a-half minute film in the Bug's Life Theater stars Flik and Hopper and is a 3D film. Some say that since the show has special effects that you can touch, it really makes it a 4D experience. Of the 3D experiences, "It's Tough to be a Bug!®" is the most intense and frightening for kids. Originally

Photo by Debbie Smith

While this attraction is hidden in DCA, it's the icon for Disney's Animal Kingdom. At Walt Disney World, when you see the "Tree of Life," know that the "It's Tough to be a Bug!®" show is housed inside.

developed for the Animal Kingdom Park in Florida, the attraction first appeared in 1998.

The show is inspired by the full-length computer-animated Pixar film *A Bug's Life,* also released in 1998.

TREASURE & TRIVIA

What is the room occupancy in the Bug Show lobby? When you were given glasses, you passed right under a rock that tells you. It's 432 and carved in stone.

TREASURE & TRIVIA

Walt Disney released the film *It's Tough to be a Bird* on December 10, 1969. The film was part live-action and cartoon and was directed by Ward Kimball. This popular short won an Academy Award for Best Short Subject. The film title was tweaked a bit for the attraction.

HIDDEN MICKEY

In the lobby waiting room for It's Tough to be a Bug!® find the Barefoot in the Bark and Web Side Story posters. Beneath and in between them you'll see two rocks that make up the ears and a large hole that make up the head. You have found a Hidden Mickey.

TREASURE & TRIVIA

A lot of joke show titles are created from some classic theater productions in the Bug's Life Theater. If you have time, you can read about some fun bug facts on the posters. Can you name the Broadway shows for each?

Little Shop of Hoppers / *Little Shop of Horrors* (Off-Broadway 1982, Broadway revival 2003) Book & lyrics by Howard Ashman, music by Alan Menken

Grass Menagerie / *The Glass Menagerie* (1945) Written by Tennessee Williams

My Fair Lady Bug / *My Fair Lady* (1956) adapted from "Pygmalion" by George Bernard Shaw (1912). Book & lyrics by Alan Jay Lerner, music by Frederick Loewe, starring Julie Andrews (Disney Legend 1991)

Antie / *Annie* (1977) Book by Thomas Meehan, lyrics by Martin Charnin, music by Charles Strouse, based on "Little Orphan Annie" by Harold Gray

Beauty & the Bees / *Beauty and the Beast* (1994) Music by Alan Menken, lyrics by Howard Ashman and Tim Rice, book by Linda Woolverton

A Cockroach Line / *A Chorus Line* (1975) Produced by Joseph Papp, book by James Kirkwood and Nicholas Dante, music by Marvin Hamlisch, lyrics by Edward Kleban

Web Side Story / *West Side Story* (1957) Book by Arthur Laurents, music by Leonard Bernstein, lyrics by Stephen Sondheim, conceived, directed and choreographed by Jerome Robbins

Barefoot in the Bark / *Barefoot in the Park* (1963) Written by Neil Simon

A Stinkbug Named Desire / *A Streetcar Named Desire* (1947) Written by Tennessee Williams, directed by Elia Kazan

The Dung and I / *The King and I* (1951) Music by Richard Rodgers, lyrics and book by Oscar Hammerstein II, based on the novel "Anna and the King of Siam" by Margaret Landon

TREASURE & TRIVIA

Question: Of all the play titles, which one is a Disney Broadway show? Answer: *Beauty and the Beast.*

HIDDEN MICKEY

Once you enter the theater, notice the second set of entrance doors, closest to the stage. In the ceiling are some strange little round plants that have hollowed out circles. One set of the plants makes a perfect Hidden Mickey.

FLIK'S "FUN" FAIR

This area opened October 6, 2002. This land was added after the Park had been open a year and a half. The area was inspired by the 1998 animated Pixar film *A Bug's Life* directed by John Lasseter. Imagineers geared this play area to children as if they had stepped into the film. Everything in the area is oversized. Kathy Mangum created the area designs, and as you enter through a giant cereal box you end up in a forest of clovers. Flik's "Fun" Fair area fills one-and-a-half acres. The atmosphere is as if you have been reduced to the size of a bug. The

Guests will get a new perspective as they enter Flik's "Fun" Fair. This area is presented by Kodak. Notice how the ripped film box, the straw and pencil are used to make you feel bug-sized?

benches are made of Popsicle sticks, and fireflies light the pathways. The building with the restrooms looks like an upside-down tissue box.

John Lasseter graduated from California Institute of the Arts. His first job for Disney was as a Jungle Cruise skipper at Disneyland.

TREASURE & TRIVIA

Instead of a Hidden Mickey, the cereal box has a Hidden Woody from *Toy Story*. Notice the pattern on the sleeve of the cowboy holding the spoon. You may pick up this clue because it says "Cowboy Crunchies." You may also see Woody on the proof of purchase, too.

John A. Lasseter was born in Hollywood on January 12, 1957. He is an animator and chief creative executive at Pixar Animation Studios. As one of the founding members of Pixar, he oversees all of their films and associated projects as an executive producer. He personally directed *Toy Story, A Bug's Life, Toy Story 2*, and *Cars*. Lasseter won two Academy Awards for Best Animated Short Film (*Tin Toy*) and a Special Achievement Award for *Toy Story*.

John Lasseter started his career in animation at Walt Disney Productions, which invented the animated feature, and Lucasfilm Computer Graphics Group, and he has now returned to Disney as the company's chief creative executive. When Pixar merged with the Walt Disney Company in April 2006, John was appointed chief creative officer for both the Pixar and Disney animation studios. He was also named Principal Creative Advisor at Walt Disney Imagineering, where he will help design attractions for Disney's theme parks.

Notice the sleeve of the Cowboy Crunchies box. Recognize it as Woody from Toy Story?

Flik's Flyers: Guests sit in gondolas and are lifted into the air by a zeppelin that has been stitched together from leaves. The idea is that Flik built it himself. In the movie, he's always making things from junk. The gondolas resemble animal cracker boxes, a box of raisins, apple juice or Chinese food take-out cartons.

The flying machine is quite clever, with a pie tin in the center and a Cool Whip®-like container, appropriately named "Whip a Whirl."

Flik's Flyers look as though Flik designed it and built it himself.

TREASURE & TRIVIA

In the Pixar film, Dave Foley provided the voice of Flik. David loaned his voice to the Flik's flyers as well. You'll also hear Dave's voice in the "It's Tough to be a Bug®" attraction. Actor Kevin Spacey gave Hopper his voice.

The animators at Pixar love John Ratzenberger. Most people recognize him as Cliff from the television show *Cheers*. In every Pixar film he has a speaking role; in *A Bug's Life* he gives P.T. Flea his voice.

Do you remember which character he played in *Toy Story* and *Toy Story 2*? He was Hamm (the piggy bank). In *Monsters, Inc.* he was Yeti The Abominable Snowman.

In *Finding Nemo* he gave the sting ray at the fish school a voice.

In *The Incredibles* he was the new villain in the end named the Under-miner. And in *Cars* he's the voice of Mack.

Speaking of fleas, did you know that fleas can jump 200 times their body length? This would be equivalent to a human clearing a 70-story building.

Francis' LadyBug Boogie is named for *A Bug's Life* cranky and defensive male ladybug character. Under a canopy of lanterns, the Francis-shaped cars twist and spin like the Mad Tea Party in a clever figure eight. Although it's not a real song, you might enjoy the prop at the entrance. It's a broken record: Ladybug Boogie–he's no lady.

Photo by Debbie Smith

TREASURE & TRIVIA

Denis Leary gave Francis a voice in the animated film. Denis is an actor, comedian, producer who you may recognize as Lt. David Poole from *Operation Dumbo Drop*, Fad King in *Wag the Dog* or Detective Michael McCann in *The Thomas Crowne Affair.*

TREASURE & TRIVIA

Did you know that the ladybug is the state insect for Delaware, Iowa, Massachusetts, New Hampshire, New York, Ohio and Tennessee?

Heimlich's Chew Chew Train is a caterpillar-shaped train. Heimlich is known for eating everything in sight and is an oversized caterpillar. He has eaten his way through a piece of watermelon and a candy valley. Imagineers piped in aromas of watermelon and vanilla cookies. When you ride it, you'll hear lots of puns in the Chew Chew Train.

Don't take a nutrition lesson from Heimlich. He thinks candy corn qualifies as a vegetable.

TREASURE & TRIVIA

Joe Ranft gives the caterpillar Heimlich his voice. In fact, you'll hear his voice in a lot of other Pixar films. He's not always a main character, but you may want to listen closely in *Toy Story* and *Toy Story 2*. (He is more noticeable as Wheezy the Penguin in *Toy Story 2*) In *Finding Nemo* he is Jacques the French Fish, and he provided additional voices in *Monsters, Inc.* and *The Incredibles*. Joe Ranft was a story supervisor who worked for Pixar. Sadly, in 2005, he died in an auto accident near Mendocino, Calif.

BUG BAG: A man told his pet millipede to get the mail. After two days, still no mail and still no pet. After looking around, he found his pet was still at the door putting on his shoes.

Photo by Debbie Smith

Princess Dot Puddle Park: A huge garden hose makes a watery play area. Here the fountains create jumping water where children love to get wet. If you don't want to jump in, it's fun to watch.

TREASURE & TRIVIA

A young actress Hayden Panettiere plays Dot in the animated film *A Bug's Life*.

TREASURE & TRIVIA

There is one lucky four-leaf clover among the clover shade in Flik's area. The clovers provide additional shade and give the feeling that while in bug's land you're only the size of an insect. Go to the churro stand and look up! If the churro stand is not out, look across the walkway between Flik's Flyers and Francis' Ladybug Boogie; you should have no problem finding it.

LESSON TO LEARN

Why are four-leaf clovers lucky? The superstition is believed to go back before Christianity. Clovers were used as a Celtic charm. Although the first literary reference to four-leaf clovers was written by Sir John Melton in 1620, when he wrote:

"If a man walking in the fields find any four-leafed grass, he shall in a small while after find some good thing."

On average, there are 10,000 three-leaf clovers for every instance of a true four-leaf clover.

Bumper bugs modeled after Tuck and Roll.

Photo by Debbie Smith

Tuck and Roll's Drive 'em Buggies:

Under the big top belonging to P.T. Flea, which looks like a recycled umbrella, kids bump around in bumper cars. Tuck and Roll are pill bug acrobats from the Bug's Life film who, well, tuck and roll. Straws are used as pillars, and fireflies hold onto suckers to light the way. Even broken pencils have a use in the area (they light the paths).

TREASURE & TRIVIA

Both characters Tuck and Roll are voiced by Michael McShane. How do you tell the two bugs apart? There are two "l"s in the name Roll, and Roll has two eyebrows.

BUG BAG: What kind of ant walks on two legs? Your Aunt.

BUG BAG: What is a tick's favorite game? Tick Tac Toe.

BUG BAG: What do termites say when a house is on fire? "Are you hungry for barbeque tonight?"

BUG BAG: Why do bees hum? Because they don't know the words.

BUG BAG: What is the best kind of computer bug? Spiders, because they make the best "Web sites."

TREASURE & TRIVIA

The oldest order of insects is the cockroach, dating back 300 million years.

The Sun Wheel is 168 feet in diameter and from this angle the boarding area is invisible.

Paradise Pier

Paradise Pier is based on the seaside boardwalks of yesteryear, such as the Long Beach Pike, Santa Cruz Beach Boardwalk and Pacific Ocean Park. It's a tribute to the 1900s amusement parks featuring nostalgic thrill rides located around the waterfront, but with a modern twist. Although similar to the carnival nostalgia, the rides of yesteryear didn't have technology to create some of the thrills that Paradise Pier provides. At night, Paradise Pier is transformed into a thing of beauty. Thousands of tiny lights illuminate the towers, wheels and décor, creating one of the most beautiful views of the resort.

The lagoon holds 16 million gallons of water. A computer-controlled wave machine creates different kinds of waves. There

Photo by Debbie Smith

California Screamin' makes its one loop in front of the giant Mickey icon. Not really a Hidden Mickey, but still fun to spot.

are 30 three-foot-wide paddles under Avalon Cove. It took about nine weeks to tune them to provide a virtual force of nature. To get the best feeling of the waves, ride California Screamin' because the waves threaten to splash you before take-off.

HIDDEN MICKEY

In the Treasures in Paradise store, there are a lot of carousel decorations. Look for the lions on the display fixtures. They have a Hidden Mickey painted as clasps on the saddles.

OPENING DAY ATTRACTION

CALIFORNIA SCREAMIN'

Designed to look like an old wooden roller coaster, California Screamin' is actually made of 5.8 million pounds of steel. A linear-induction launch system catapults guests from zero to 55 mph in less than five seconds before reaching the first hill. California Screamin' is the roller coaster with the longest track in California more than a mile long at 6,072 feet. The peak is 120 feet high with a maximum drop of 108 feet at a 50 degree angle. California Screamin' has a full inverted loop of 360 degrees around a stylized Mickey Mouse. There are 108 speakers, including those mounted in the passenger cars,

with a modern soundtrack created for every turn, twist and loop.

TREASURE & TRIVIA

The name California Screamin' is a pun off the song *California Dreamin'*, which was recorded by The Mamas and The Papas. The song was written by John and Michelle Phillips. You might hear the song in the background.

Photo by Debbie Smith

Riders on California Screamin' are called, "Screamers."

TREASURE & TRIVIA

The blue tubes covering the track are for screaming. The Imagineers felt that in order to be good neighbors they wanted to limit the sounds for the hotels and residents nearby. The tubes keep guests' voices from traveling too far outside the Park.

The world's first roller coasters were sleds on man-made ice hills in 15th century Russia. In the winter, children and adults would trek up 70 feet of stairs to climb onto a straw seat and fly down the hill. In 1804, the idea of the "Russian Mountains" was brought to Paris for the World's Fair. Small wheels were added to the track and thrill seekers had a new hobby. Thirteen years later, the "Russian Mountains" in Paris added locking wheels, continuous tracks and eventually cables that hoisted cars to the top of the hill.

LESSON TO LEARN

The old saying, "What goes up, must come down" is not only true for roller coasters but is a physics law that puts the "coast" in roller coaster. We call it the law of gravity. Typically, roller coasters start with a big drop to give the train enough momentum to sustain the entire ride. Positive gravitational forces, "G-forces," press you into your seat when you're at the bottom of the dip; that's why it's difficult to raise your hand through the loop. So called "negative G's" create the sense of weightlessness as you crest over the top of the hill and make you feel like you can pop out of your seat.

Photo by Debbie Smith

King Arthur Carousel is in Disneyland, so the Little Mermaid's Dad, King Triton, has this Carousel named for him in DCA.

OPENING DAY ATTRACTION

KING TRITON'S CAROUSEL

This merry-go-round was inspired by the film *The Little Mermaid*. Ariel's father, King Triton, watches over it to be sure all the marine life is well behaved. Each of the 56 sea creatures are hand painted and unique. Who wouldn't want to ride a sea horse, whale, dolphin, otter, seal or fish? These animals were chosen because they're all native to the California Coast.

The merry-go-round system was purchased from the D.H. Morgan Manufacturing Company in La Selva Beach, California. The plant is just south of San Francisco. Although the sea creatures were designed by Disney Imagineers, they were built by Morgan Manufacturing. There are 56 sea creatures and two water chariots on the merry-go-round. The ride lasts about a minute-and-a-half and can accommodate 2,448 people per hour.

Instead of "gay 90s" music, the merry-go-round plays 1960 Beach Boys tunes and surf songs with a band-organ treatment.

TREASURE & TRIVIA

The orange-colored garibaldi fish is the official state saltwater fish of California.

Although King Triton's Carousel is new, the Imagineers wanted to give tribute to the California boardwalks of the past. They've honored 16 of them with medallions on the outside of the merry-go-round. The Santa Monica Pier still exists and so does the Santa Cruz Beach Boardwalk. The honored boardwalks are:

- **The Pike,** Long Beach 1905 to 1979
- **Lick Pier,** Ocean Park 1923 to 1924
- **Santa Monica Pier,** Santa Monica 1923 to present
- **Venice of America,** Venice Beach 1904
- **Nu Pike,** Long Beach 1950
- **Virginia Park,** Long Beach 1939
- **Fraser's Million Dollar Pier,** Ocean Park 1911 to 1912
- **Abbott Kiney,** Venice 1905 to 1920
- **Looff's Pier,** Santa Monica 1908
- **Playland at the Beach,** San Francisco 1928
- **Ocean Park Pier,** Ocean Park 1920
- **Santa Cruz Boardwalk,** Santa Cruz 1902 to present
- **Venice Pier,** Venice 1925
- **Belmont Park,** San Diego 1925
- **Pickering Pleasure Pier,** Ocean Park 1920 to 1924
- **Pop, Pacific Ocean Park,** Santa Monica 1955 to 1967

Walt Disney and his staff visited many of these piers and studied them before building Disneyland. Many of them suggested to Walt that his idea would fail without the Midway and that it would be too expensive to keep it clean. Walt's instincts were right.

TREASURE & TRIVIA

Look for the medallion for Looff's Pier. Charles I.D. Looff (1852 to 1918) was one of the original carousel manufacturers. He built 17 for himself, and a total of 40 all together. He operated carousels in Santa Cruz, Santa Monica, Redondo Beach, Venice Beach, Ocean Park and Playland in San Francisco, Calif.

Pictured here is Santa Monica Pier which is still in operation today.

OPENING DAY ATTRACTION

THE MIDWAY

This is a classic amusement area with food, games and souvenirs. Typical of the pre-World War II boardwalks, it recreates the feeling of an amusement pier. At the time of printing, if you wanted one person to play all seven games at least once, it would cost less than $20. One game guarantees you win, so it might be worth stopping by.

HIDDEN MICKEY

At the end of the board-walk is Paradise Pier Mural. Notice the Mickey Mouse-shaped balloon the child is holding.

BOARDWALK BOWL

The best deal at the boardwalk; you bowl six balls for $1. It's a little tough to score high enough to win a prize, buy everyone in the family can pretty much play and enjoy the game.

Boardwalk Bowl was featured in an episode of the television show The Bachelor one season.

Find your alma mater's flag if you graduated from a California University.

SHORE SHOT

For $2 you get one basketball to toss in the hoop. Like most carnival games, it seems the hoop is a little smaller than regulation size. The cool thing about this booth is the tribute to all the state colleges. All the California Universities have their banners hanging. If you're a graduate of a state university, see if you can find your alma mater. When the Park opened, this game was called Reboundo Beach Basketball, a pun on Redondo Beach. However, the new Shore Shot décor offers a better theme.

SAN JOAQUIN VOLLEY

Here players get two softballs for $2 to throw and land in the raffia basket. The cast member will show you that a back spin on the toss increases your chances. The San

Everyone wins a prize at New Haul Fishery!

Joaquin Valley is where most of the fruits and vegetables are grown in California. The name San Joaquin Volley pokes fun at the name but keeps the agricultural theme.

NEW HAUL FISHERY

This game is popular because for $2 every fisher-person wins a prize. The size of the prize depends on the random marking on the bottom of the fish. The cast member will give you a fishing pole with a magnet on the line. The fish have magnets in their mouth. As they float by, whichever fish you land on reveals the size of your plush toy.

LESSON TO LEARN

The name is a spin off of Newhall, Calif., which is about 57 miles northwest of Anaheim. The Santa Clara River is the largest river system in Southern California and it remains in a relatively natural state. The river goes through Newhall and flows through the San Gabriel Mountains of Los Angeles County and through Ventura County. The southern steelhead trout use the river as a migration corridor, which explains why the game has pictures of southern steelhead.

HIDDEN MICKEY

Under the L in the New Haul Fishery sign there is a Hidden Mickey in the snow on the mountain.

League Baseball teams. The Walt Disney Company owned the Anaheim Angels during the 2002 season when they won the World Series. A World Series banner still hangs in the booth.

DISNEY'S ANGELS IN THE OUTFIELD

Each player pays $2 for three softballs. To win, you must throw the ball and knock down two or more catcher plaques on the back wall. The booth is decorated with a baseball theme, including banners to represent all the California Major

TREASURE & TRIVIA

ngels in the Outfield is also the title of a Disney movie starring Joseph Gordon-Levitt, Danny Glover, Brenda Fricker, Tony Danza and Christopher Lloyd.

Photo by Debbie Smith

From 1965 until 1996 the American League baseball team was called the California Angels. From 1997-2004 the team was called the Anaheim Angels. Currently the team is called, Los Angeles Angels of Anaheim.

Horse racing is too conventional for Disney's Paradise Pier, how about trying your luck at dolphin racing?

DOLPHIN DERBY

The Dolphin Derby is one of the most fun games to watch. The cast members like to have all the seats taken to ensure the biggest prize is won. There is one winner per game and players compete by rolling wooden balls into holes. Each hole has a point value associated with it and the roller's dolphin moves ahead the appropriate number of spaces. It's the only racing game on the midway. Like racehorses, the dolphins have numbers and names, so choose a favorite!

COWHUENGA PASS

For $2, a player receives two softballs to toss into a milk can. Cahuenga Pass is in California, but there probably aren't a lot of cows at the top. For fun, the play on words provides a fun fair theme with the prize-winning cows in the back. The milk cans are named for these fine heifers. The names are Millie, Betsy, Buttercup, Belle, Elsie and the ribbon winner Ed.

Unlike most carnivals, in Paradise Pier the Midway is clean and the game operators don't yell at passers by.

TREASURE & TRIVIA

On the bottom left-hand side there is a cage filled with award-winning cheese. No doubt a famous mouse has been nibbling on it, since he left his sorcerer's hat and wand.

Which two bovines share a name with a Disney animated character? Belle shares her name with the leading lady from *Beauty and the Beast*, and Ed is one of the hyenas from *Lion King*.

HIDDEN MICKEY

The face-painting booth has a couple of Hidden Mickeys. Look at the photos of the artwork; a couple of girls on the left-side panel are sporting America's favorite character.

OPENING DAY ATTRACTION

SUN WHEEL

The magnificent Sun Wheel is 168 feet in diameter and even more breathtaking at night. There are 24 gondolas that can accommodate six people. The gondolas are color coded as the 16 orange and purple cars slip and slide within the diameter of the wheel. The purple cars

The lights on the Sun Wheel flash at night and are beautiful to watch.

Photo by Debbie Smith

TREASURE & TRIVIA

This is one of only three spinning wheels of its kind in the world today. Coney Island in New York has the legendary Wonder Wheel, built in 1920, and Japan has the other.

The world's first Ferris Wheel was created by Pittsburgh, Penn. bridge builder George W. Ferris for Chicago's 1893 World's Fair. The original was supported by two 140-foot steel towers, with a 250-foot diameter and 825-foot circumference. It had 36 wooden cars that each held approximately 60 people. The Ferris Wheel grossed over $726,800 during its short time in operation at 50 cents a ride.

OPENING DAY ATTRACTION

MALIBOOMER

are designed to swing faster than the orange ones. The red cars are fixed and enjoy the view from the highest point.

The celestial face is one of the most recognizable icons for DCA. The sun wheel has a 500-foot circumference. The Sun Wheel overlooks the four-acre bay, but the boarding area is carefully hidden from a distance; from across the lagoon it looks like guests board underwater.

This attraction is based on the old high-striker strength test game: the one where the barkers would yell "swing the mallet ring the bell and win the lovely lady a prize." Only in this version, you are the projectile that rings the bell. The Maliboomer launches you 180 feet straight up in two-and-a-half seconds. There are jet lift carriages that catapult you up in less than three seconds. That's faster than 60 feet a second. As you crest the top, you'll feel it pull you back down before your momentum upward is completed. There are three towers, each with four open carriages attached to the sides. Although the ride is smooth, it surely will help circulate the adrenaline in your body.

It's fun to watch people freak out prematurely when the Maliboomer does the safety check. Several ride operators push buttons at the same time to make sure the weight is distributed equally.

The ride lifts just a few feet off the ground and a false start can torment riders.

The name is a tribute to the beautiful ocean city of Malibu, Calif. Lots of famous celebrities reside there, but it is also famous for its surfing, as seen in the *Soarin'* film. Malibu is 55 miles north of Disneyland.

Photo by Debbie Smith

Photo by Debbie Smith

Maliboomer looks like a high-striker strength test game. You climb 180 feet in less than 2 1/2 seconds.

ORANGE STINGER

This is a swing ride that operates inside of a peeling orange. There are 48 single bee swings. As the swings pick up speed, the seats take flight. You may not notice that when the ride begins a single bee drones alone, but as the swings take flight, more bees join in until the ride has a whole swarm buzzing along. The scent of fresh oranges fills the air from the center of the interior.

One of the last oranges left in Orange County, and probably the biggest!

S.S. RUSTWORTHY
(presented by McDonald's)

The Disney Myth

The S.S. Trustworthy was once a reliable fire-ship along the lagoon. After many years of service, the boat was wrecked and abandoned at the edge of Paradise Bay. The first "T" in its name has since rusted away.

Now the S.S. rustworthy is a children's water playground. Every 10 minutes, a siren goes off and a jet of watery mist bursts majestically from a boiler vent. There are two firefighter cutouts with blast hoses for kids willing to square off and get soaked. The ship allows young people to cool down and burn off energy. You may want to pack extra clothes to change into, since some of the water guns can get you really wet.

Adults and kids square off to hose each other down!

The S.S. Trustworthy rusted out and when the T wore off, it became the S.S. rustworthy.

TREASURE & TRIVIA

Notice the California flag above the S.S. rustworthy.

The only theme park to fly its own state flag is DCA. Disneyland ironically flies the Louisiana State Flag in New Orleans Square.

HIDDEN MICKEY

On the console inside the S.S. rustworthy is a Hidden Mickey using the dials. The dials don't touch, but it is still considered a Hidden Mickey.

HIDDEN MICKEY

Look for the Sorcerer Mickey antennae topper. This qualifies as a Hidden Mickey.

OPENING DAY ATTRACTION

JUMPIN' JELLYFISH

This is a very tame version of the Maliboomer. The 50-foot tower gently pulls people up and then back down again. Created to look like an underwater experience, the tower resembles kelp beds, while the ride vehicles resemble jellyfish.

Jumpin' Jellyfish has a gentle climb and fall which is fun for the little ones!

OPENING DAY ATTRACTION

MULHOLLAND MADNESS

Imagineer Tim Delaney calls Mulholland Madness, "The world's scariest slow roller coaster." Classic west coast cars, police cars, red fire engines and "flower power" vans make quick twists and turns. The name Mulholland Madness is a tribute to Mulholland Drive in a scenic 50-mile trip that winds through Los Angeles to the Pacific coastline in Malibu. One effect that makes this mouse-like steel coaster fun is that it does not bank its corners. So just as you think the car is going to go over the edge, it pivots sharply around the tight curve, whipping you around.

HIDDEN MICKEY

On the center pole closest to the S.S. rustworthy, there is a Hidden Mickey disguised in the bubbles. This one is a little tricky to find, but it's located just above the jellyfish when the vehicles are being loaded underneath two orange fish.

Look for the Disney Studios in the mural and the Mickey shaped swimming pool.

LESSON TO LEARN

William Mulholland (1855 to 1935) is a controversial civic engineer in Los Angeles history. He was obsessed with engineering a plan to deliver water from the Owens River to Los Angeles to support the city's exploding water needs. Owens River is some 200 miles away, and the farmers and residents there had their own plan for this valuable resource. For eight years, Mulholland directed thousands of workers to blast tunnels, carve sluiceways, clear roads, lay railroad track and run power lines. By 1913, the Los Angeles Aqueduct was finished. For years there would be battles between the people of Owens Valley and William Mulholland, and many times the aqueduct was sabotaged. In 1928, the St. Francis Dam gave way, releasing 12.5 billion gallons of water. The water flooded the Santa Clara Valley and moved through Oxnard and Ventura toward the Pacific Ocean. More than 500 people were killed, and everything in its way was destroyed: livestock, structures, railways, bridges and orchards. William Mulholland was blamed, as he was responsible for its chief design. No criminal charges were brought against him, but he retreated to self-isolation and died in 1935 at the age of 79.

HIDDEN MICKEY

Look at the mural next to the entrance. Notice the large red car with flames on the hood. Look carefully at the license plate to see the Hidden Mickey.

HIDDEN MICKEY

As you enter the line of the ride, look backward at the mural to find another car with another Hidden Mickey on the license plate.

HIDDEN MICKEY

Near the Alamo Rent a Car sign on the mural outside of Mulholland Madness, look for a Mickey-shaped swimming pool. The Beverly Hills area and pool on this character map is in close proximity to where Walt Disney's personal home was at: 355 N. Carolwood Drive.

TREASURE & TRIVIA

It's fun to spot the Disney studios in the mural map. Follow the 134 Highway and look for a sorcerer Mickey hat on a building. The hat-shaped building is the former feature animation studio.

OPENING DAY ATTRACTION

GOLDEN ZEPHYR

There are 6 twelve-passenger rockets that are suspended by cables from the 85 foot tower. The Zephyr spins and lifts guests into the air over Paradise Bay.

Photo by Debbie Smith

The Golden Zephyr is a different kind of merry-go-round.

TREASURE & TRIVIA

The word "zephyr" means west wind or a fast breeze.

DINOSAUR JACK SUNGLASSES SHACK

HIDDEN MICKEY

Behind the cash register there is a collage. Behind the dented hubcap there is a Hidden Mickey in the 11 o'clock position. Not a typical Hidden Mickey of three circles, but a plastic Mickey Mouse face, smiles back at you.

MIDWAY SHOPS

The Midway shops offer good merchandise in a wonderful carnival, circus-type décor. Clever puns fill the shop, so even if you're not buying, it's fun to stroll through for a couple of jokes.

Photo by Debbie Smith

POINT MUGU TATTOO

In typical Disney humor, the sign states that "All tattoos are temporary, and all sales are final." Notice on the billboard outside the shop that the man with all the tattoos has one special one. On his heart, there is a heart-shaped tattoo, which names "Lady Beard" as his love. Keep reading to find out who Lady Beard is.

HIDDEN MICKEY

On the back wall, there is a painted display at the top of the shelving. Look at the Paradise Pier logo to identify the Hidden Mickey.

HIDDEN MICKEY

Once you've found the first Hidden Mickey in the tattoo shop, turn to your left and look at the other displays on the top of the shelving. The third design from the left has a surfboard with a painted Hidden Mickey on it.

MAN HAT N' BEACH

Here Imagineers poked fun at Manhattan Beach by calling it a hat shop. One sign says, "Some hats contain rabbits."

HIDDEN MICKEY

To find this Hidden Mickey look at the display with the octopus holding the mirrors. On the back of his head you'll see some spots. One of the spots is a Hidden Mickey.

SIDE SHOW SHIRTS

The sign likes to play with any word that usually ends in "ties" by changing it to "tees." Before going into the store, notice some fun things about the outside signs.

HIDDEN MICKEY

Look for the merchandise display table with the man lying on nails. There is a hidden Mickey painted in the wood on the board below the nails, straight down from his wrist.

HIDDEN MICKEY

On the back wall there is a cute painting of a crosseyed gunsmith named Betty Ducks. On the right side of the frame, at about the 3 o'clock position of the frame, notice the Hidden Mickey.

TREASURE & TRIVIA

On the wall is a portrait of Vipera, a character who plays with snakes. Do you recognize the snake from a Disney animated film? How about Kaa from *Jungle Book*?

On the outside of the building is a large clown. Notice how the clown's eyes seem to watch you as you stroll along the planks.

Lastly, see Lady Beard on the marquis outside the store. Another marquis (look at the tattoos) tells us that she may be having a love affair with another of the Midway characters.

A nice view of Ariel's Grotto, a character dining experience.

Chapter 7

Grand Californian Hotel & Spa

Although the Disneyland Hotel has a lot of Disney history, when the Grand Californian was built, it was clear that it wanted to earn flagship status. Peter Dominick was the senior principal architect on the Grand Californian project. The hotel was inspired by and designed in the Craftsman style with many Arts and Crafts details. Reminiscent of National Park lodges, the Grand Californian is almost an attraction unto itself. Just as the National Park lodges were intended to maximize the views and grandeur of their surroundings, the Grand Californian takes advantage of its premier location and the views that surround it. Complete with amazing views of Disney's California Adventure, the hotel is nestled in between the Park and Downtown Disney. The Grand Californian even has its own entrance into DCA.

Once California's history, culture and heritage was set as the new theme for the Park,

HIDDEN MICKEY

Study carefully the emblem for the Grand Californian. In the middle of the giant sequoia (redwood tree) is a Hidden Mickey. Once you recognize it, you'll see this Hidden Mickey everywhere, making it difficult to count all the Hidden Mickeys.

Imagineers set out to review all of the state's architectural styles. Executive Vice President of Walt Disney Imagineering Wing Chao oversaw the planning, architecture and design for the hotel. Discovering that there were no large, commercial Arts and Crafts hotels, "gave us the energy, the reason to do something unique and different" he says. Not only had no one built an Arts and Crafts hotel before, but it would also blend nicely with the Grizzly Peak Recreation Area of DCA. Disney is a company who has built its reputation on incorporating

The sliding stained glass doors feature Grizzly Peak and are breath taking.

the smallest details. "Arts and Crafts is all about the details, joints, connections, patterns," Wing Chao says. "And we like to surprise guests with the 'wow' effect."

The "wow" effect begins as you enter the building. The two sliding stained glass doors come together to create a single image of DCA's Grizzly Peak and the hotel emblem.

The dancing bears on the apron of the registration desk.

Although the doors are magnificent from the outside, looking at them from inside the hotel with the sun shining behind them is even more breathtaking.

Susan Dannenfelser created the tile murals on the apron of the front desk. There are 29 bears in the ceramic tiles, each representing a person involved in the hotel project. The bears are all in a dancing pose. Bear number 20 (from the front left) is the "everyone bear." "That way everyone who points to Bear 20 can say, 'That's me.'" Bear 6, 7, and 8 represent the artist at two different ages and her husband Kirk Beck, who also worked on the hotel. Susan also sculpted the gargoyle-like birds that stand guard at the elevators.

TREASURE & TRIVIA

A bit harder to find, there is one hidden pixie in the ceramic tiles on the apron of the front desk. Some say it's Tinker Bell; others say it's a pixie, but you decide. Count from the left side, four ceramic pine trees. She is in the right corner between trees three and four. The tile is green and it's more of a silhouette angle.

Parker Blake was commissioned to create the tapestries behind the front desk.

GREAT HALL LOBBY

As you enter the Great Hall, you'll appreciate its massive beams, vaulted ceiling and warm earthen hues. Some Arts and Crafts purists may protest the use of simulated rock, fiberglass beams and other contemporary materials at the Grand Californian Hotel, but contemporary materials are critical when dealing with contemporary matters such as building maintenance, building codes, fire codes and guest safety. Even after making those concessions, the results are true to the Craftsman style where "form follows function." More than half of the 144,000-square-foot complex is open to the public; the results are amazingly opulent.

LESSON TO LEARN

The phrase "form follows function" is often used in describing Craftsman style architecture, furniture and decoration. For example, if a piece of furniture requires a hinge, make the hinge beautiful and part of the style of the furniture.

The concrete hearth is more than three stories tall. The inglenook is large enough to walk into, sit by the fire and warm up from the cool California evenings. There are plenty of rocking chairs for adults and children in the hearth, which is a little like a cave, making it warm and cozy. At specified times, cast members come sit in this area to share stories with younger guests. Families often sit in the hearth and quietly unwind from the adventures of the Disneyland Resort.

When you're in the lobby and looking back at the hearth, The Grand Californian Hotel logo of the sequoia and Hidden Mickey are imprinted in the top corners.

The California poppy graces the marble floor and carpeting with a perfect continuation of pattern. Notice how the Imagineers designed the poppies on the floor to be closed, because the flowers are indoors and naturally the sun can't open them there. Custom light fixtures, old-style phones and craftsman-style furniture make the hotel rich in details. The Great Hall is a wonderful place to sit and relax while waiting to meet people or come to listen to the piano player, or read a favorite book.

TREASURE & TRIVIA

Martinware Pottery (1873 to 1923) is a distinctive type of stoneware from the 1870s through the First World War. Considered a good example of Victorian art, Martinware is best known for bird sculptures and bowls. In London, there were four brothers: Robert who trained as a sculptor, Walter who was the firm's specialist on the wheel, Edward whose work included mostly fish and floral designs and Charles who ran the shop. They usually used salt-glaze stoneware, a high-temperature firing method where salt is thrown into the kiln to fuse to the clay and create a rough surface.

Take time to enjoy the rich details, such as the cabinets that grace the lobby with many examples of books, pottery, dishware and other inspirational resources for the hotel. The front desk lamps are from Royal Tiffany. The Arts and Crafts details are even on the metal elevator faceplates, doors and cabinetry hardware created by Craftsmen Hardware Company.

The bird sculptures perched in the corners of the main areas were made by Susan Dannenfelser in the style of Martinware Pottery.

TREASURE & TRIVIA

I f you stand on the third floor with your back to the lobby, notice the bird on the right side has a slicked-back feather and has been nicknamed Elvis.

Photo by Debbie Smith

HIDDEN MICKEY

The grandfather clock was a joint creation of Warren Hile and Michael Ashford. This style of clock is available for sale in catalogs, except notice this one has a Hidden Mickey in the slight indentation on the face of the clock in the Great Hall.

HEARTHSTONE LOUNGE

Notice how the grains of the wood match in the Hearthstone Lounge. This is because the lounge is paneled from a single fallen coastal redwood tree. The room was intended to look like a mens' smoking lounge. Since California law prohibits smoking indoors, everyone can enjoy this quiet sanctuary. Mens' smoking lounges are typically dark, but Imagineers wanted women to feel comfortable here too. To accommodate the fairer sex, the artwork was created en "plein air" style and only features women. The artwork was commissioned by Parker Blake of Englewood, Colorado.

Photo by Debbie Smith

Artist Jeff Brundage carved the centerpiece of the bar. The quote sets the tone for the en plein air atmosphere.

 LESSON TO LEARN

What is en plein air? The French translation is "in the open air." Until the late 1700s, it was not acceptable for artists to leave their studios to paint. Painting landscapes outdoors was considered low brow and discouraged. Although landscapes were always incorporated into portraits, it was not considered a suitable subject by itself. Artists eventually began to venture outside to learn from what they saw in nature. They noticed how weather, light and movement had significant impact. Today, en plein air is not just a style, but a location where artists paint. Modern en plein air will appreciate landscapes, but may include portraits. Plein air does not limit itself to the type of media; it can include oil, acrylic, pastel or watercolor.

Once you understand the en plein air inspiration and theme, the wood engraving above the bar makes more sense: "Nature is the source of all artistic expression."

Artist Jeff Brundage carved the centerpiece of the coffee bar in Hearthstone Lounge. The Missouri-born artist also made the carvings in the Storyteller's Cafe.

HIDDEN MICKEY

Notice the Hidden Mickey as part of the decoration on each of the light fixtures in Hearthstone Lounge. You'll see Mickey even on the wall sconces.

HIDDEN MICKEY

Check out the painting in the nook to the left near the serving station and to the left of the door. The painting is of a woman holding a paintbrush and looking at an art easel. The frame has a Hidden Mickey in the lower right-hand corner.

GUEST ROOMS & SUITES

There are 751 guest rooms in the Grand Californian Hotel and 38 suites. Standard guest rooms are 353 square feet and have wood furnishings, carved headboards, an Italian marble vanity, leaded glass lights and beautiful views. Some rooms have private balconies. There are Hidden Mickeys, classic animation cells, but all the décor is subtle and sophisticated. If you request it, a few rooms even have bunk beds.

There are four styles of artisan suites, including one format with queen size beds and three variations with king size beds. The 34

One of the three pools at Disney's Grand Californian Hotel.

artisan suites range from 694 to 793 square feet depending on their configuration and all enjoy balcony views. You can entertain 25 to 35 people in the suites, and they all enjoy concierge floor privileges.

There are two vice presidential suites: the Arcadia and the Arroyo. Each provides 1,604 square feet of comfort. Each suite is complete with a balcony view of Disney's California Adventure Park, a fireplace, room to entertain 50 people, a dining room, living room and service pantry, separate from the sleeping area with a king size bed. They can also connect with an artisan suite if needed.

There are also two presidential suites: the El Capitan and Mount Whitney suites, each with over 1,990 square feet. Both suites are large enough to entertain 75 people with a fireplace, dining area, a kitchen service area, a king size bed in the sleeping area and a large balcony view of Disney's California Adventure and the pool area. Although the El Capitan suite has the larger space, the Mount Whitney suite has an extra fireplace, dining area and private office. All four suites are adorned with Craftsman style furniture, lamps and elegance. Thomas Stangeland's furniture is seen in the dining area. The suite's living room is Disney's interpretation of a contemporary Gamble House.

 ## LESSON TO LEARN

The hotel and suites are designed in the Greene and Greene style, named for brothers and architects Charles Sumner Greene (1868-1957) and Henry Mather Greene (1870 to 1954). They both had a strong love of nature and incorporated it into their designs. They had also studied woodworking, metalworking and tool making early in their careers and learned to incorporate this into their designs. By 1902 to 1910, the Greene Brothers' office was at its peak. Working primarily in residential homes, they designed more than 150 projects in this period. One of their most famous buildings is the Gamble House in Pasadena, Calif. You might recognize this house from the movies. It was used in the 1985 film *Back to the Future,* starring Michael J. Fox and Christopher Lloyd. The outside of the Gamble House in Pasadena is featured in the movie as Dr. Emmett Brown's house.

LESSON TO LEARN

The Gamble House was designed in 1908 by architects Greene and Greene. It was commissioned by Mr. and Mrs. David Berry Gamble as a summer home in Pasadena. Mr. Gamble was a second generation member of the Procter and Gamble Company in Cincinnati. The house and its furnishings were designed to incorporate many art pieces owned by the family. Tours are available if you'd like to visit. Go to www.gamblehouse.org for more information.

LESSON TO LEARN

Another great architect, Frank Lloyd Wright (1869 to 1959), also inspired the style of the hotel. Wright was an American architect whose impact on design is incalculable. He was known for designing public buildings and private homes, and all the details that go into them. His glass design and furniture were decades ahead of his time. He was endlessly fascinated by the challenge of "form follows function." Frank Lloyd Wright was originally trained as a civil engineer and he worked as a draftsman until 1893. A couple of his most famous works are Fallingwater house in Pennsylvania and the Guggenheim Museum in New York City.

MANDARA SPA

Formerly the Eureka Springs Spa, the new, larger area features a fitness center, steam rooms and nail spa, that offers a variety of facials, massages, wraps, pedicures, manicures and even teeth whitening. The spa offers treatments for every member of the family, including pregnant women, teens and youths. The spa is decorated in a Balinese style, which surprisingly blends well with the Arts and Crafts style of the hotel. Mandara Spa is known for operating spas in 54 resorts and more than 120 cruise ships. They begin with an exotic relaxation area for the tea ceremony, which is an ancient Zen Buddhist tradition that gives a calm and relaxed feeling to separate you from the excitement outside.

For appointments and pricing, call 714-300-7350. You can also check out their website at www.mandaraspa.com.

POOL AND GROUNDS

Good examples of "form follows function" are the beautiful gates designed by Tim Burrows that

Photo by Debbie Smith

Stop to appreciate these magnificent gates with flowers, the sun and large insects made of iron.

adorn the pool. Nature is the source for inspiration. He uses the sun, moon, flowers and even insects. His gates also adorn the pathway to Downtown Disney, with the moon shining through the trees. You may

recognize his work again on the fire screens in the lobby as well.

There are three pools and two hot tubs for guests. The turtle fountain pool has an oversized turtle who replenishes the water. This lap pool is good for water workouts or sunbathing and is usually the quieter of the two pools. Families may enjoy either pool together although children would rather play at the Redwood Pool.

The Redwood pool is more for the children or children at heart with a 100-foot water slide that circles around the stump of a giant fallen redwood. Through the fence you may see the Redwood Creek Challenge area of Disney's California Adventure Park.

Photo by Debbie Smith

The turtle fountain plays with guests as it spits in the pool.

Kids love the Redwood pool slide.

There is also a Mickey Mouse-shaped pool for the little children to splash and play.

On the opposite side of the hotel near the convention center is Brisa Courtyard. This area is graced with the monorail traveling quietly through it and is lined with more than 90 sequoia trees.

CONVENTION CENTER

The convention center has 20,000 square feet of rental space, including the Sequoia ballroom with 12,000 square feet. There are 18 breakout rooms named mostly for flowers, and seven of them have their own access to an outdoor terrace for break areas.

To book conventions, call 714-956-6510.

HIDDEN MICKEY

In the Sequoia South Foyer as you pass the restrooms, ATM and phones, the first painting closest to the Trillium Room has a Hidden Mickey in the corners of the frame. The painting is a landscape of a coastal scene.

DINING

There are three places to get a meal at the Grand Californian Hotel. The locals like White Water Snacks, which is near the pool and offers both hot and cold sandwiches. The other two are full-service restaurants: the Storyteller's Cafe and Napa Rose. It is strongly suggested since both restaurants are so popular that you call ahead for priority seating at 714-781-3463.

Storyteller's Cafe is also a favorite among the locals. A bowl of their corn chowder or the prime rib buffet makes the wait worth it. The restaurant is designed in the Mission style of architecture, with a contemporary feel. Outside the restaurant there are epigrams that fit in with the hotel theme: "Hearth & Home," "The life so short the craft so long to learn" and "By hammer

Be sure to try the corn chowder, it's delicious.

and hands do all things stand."

On a pillar in the waiting area, there is a tribute to the restaurant designer Marty Dorf. The epigram was written by Elbert Hubbard and says, "One machine can do the work of fifty ordinary men. No machine can do the work of one extraordinary man." The last projects that Dorf designed before his death were Storyteller's Cafe and Napa Rose. Dorf is also known for designing the California Grill restaurant at the top of the Contemporary Resort at Walt Disney World, Citricos restaurant at the Grand Floridian Resort and Palo restaurant on both the Disney Magic and Disney Wonder cruise ships.

The Cafe complements the rest of the hotel with some beautiful artwork worth noticing. As you enter the restaurant, you'll notice the tile mural above the buffet of a little boy reading. This Storyteller's Cafe mural was created by Motawi

The orignial concept of the restaurant included stories about the paintings seen here.

Tileworks and with an appropriate tribute to Walt Disney celebrating him as the greatest storyteller of all time. In the background you'll see Sleeping Beauty Castle (Disneyland's castle) and Tinker Bell.

TREASURE & TRIVIA

The tile mural is inspired by a Gladding McBean & Company piece called "A Child's Storybook World" first created in 1927. The original is forty 6"x 6" tiles in the Robin Hood Room at the Wilmington Public Library in Wilmington, Calif.

The original concept for Storyteller's Cafe was that while you would wait for your meal, your server would share with you a story depicted in one of the paintings on the wall. Sadly, the staff was pulled in two different directions, telling stories and serving food. Since the cafe is foremost a restaurant, the storytelling had to be phased out. You can still enjoy the beautiful paintings depicting some of California's greatest tales. One of the best remnants of this idea is embossed in the floor as you enter, "Storyteller's Cafe, Let us provide you with food and drink, as you embark on your journey through California folklore. The storyteller awaits. Listen and enjoy."

LESSON TO LEARN

There are seven 6-foot murals depicting great stories about California. Imagineers sifted through many stories, but depicted these moments from seven famous stories. Each was chosen to evoke a sense of discovery through literature. Although it is not known who the artists are, the murals were painted in the style of *Treasure Island* illustrator N.C. Wyeth. Even the music played in the restaurant is inspired by the story murals. If you don't recognize any of them, try reading:

- *The Cruise of the Dazzler* by Jack London
- *The Mark of Zorro* by Johnston McCulley
- *Tortilla Flat* by John Steinbeck
- *The Californians* by Gertrude Atherton
- *Ahwahnee Tale* (a Miwok Indian Legend) author unknown
- *The Celebrated Jumping Frog of Calaveras County* by Mark Twain
- *Island of the Blue Dolphins* by Scott O'Dell

For a quick synopsis of the stories that accommodate the paintings, look in the appendix.

The California Gold Rush is the eighth story and is depicted in the faux bronze cut-outs.

There are different styles of

lamps, including the bean-pot style in the seating area and the California Gold Rush lanterns. Around the fireplaces and booths are tiles of children reading. There are 19 of each to represent the early 1900s, when the Arts and Crafts Movement was at its peak. The artists used a traditional plaster-press-mold technique and a special glaze called "sea foam." The kitchen tiles with the letters A-B-C-D-E were designed in the Arts and Crafts movement lettering style.

While waiting for your table, you may sit in the hand-carved, quarter-sawn oak benches. Each depicts a child reading a book. Small iron books grace the corners of the booths with phrases such as "Storyteller's Cafe: with each new adventure a story begins."

For breakfast, Storyteller's Cafe hosts a character meal with Chip n' Dale in the mornings. For dinner, kids usually like to create their own pizzas. Reservations are available by calling 714- 956-6755.

Mackintosh Jewelry can be found with a similar rose logo to Napa Rose in the Frank Lloyd Wright catalog.

Photo by Debbie Smith

NAPA ROSE

Napa Rose is the premier restaurant of the Grand Californian. It is decorated in the rich style of the Arts and Crafts Movement. The art glass was made using equipment from a defunct Tiffany firm. The room is filled with light-colored woods, a romantic fire pit, 20-foot-high vaulted ceilings and a showcase wine cellar that holds 600 vintages. The cellar features a "Wall of Fame" with magnums of premium California wines, available for purchase. Many of the bottles have been signed by California's winemakers.

The restaurant seats 237 guests and features a display kitchen and a 78-seat lounge. Guests throughout the restaurant look out through floor-to-ceiling windows that provide a dramatic view of nearby Grizzly Peak.

The logo for Napa Rose is inspired by the rose motif drawings, architecture and interiors of Charles Rennie Mackintosh.

Photo by Debbie Smith

The Napa Rose style is Glasgow, named for Glasgow, Scotland but made famous by designer Charles Rennie Mackintosh.

 ## TREASURE & TRIVIA

 ## LESSON TO LEARN

The name Napa Rose comes from the tradition of planting a rose bush at the end of the row of vines in the vineyard. The rose is more sensitive to weather and pests than the grapevines and is a good indicator to what may shortly affect the vines. The rose also attracts bees, which help pollinate the grape buds. Ironically, the muralist was not told of this tradition and painted Napa Valley without the roses at the end of the vine row.

Charles Rennie Mackintosh is a prolific and creative innovator of the Glasgow style which evolved at the turn of the 20th century. He lived in Glasgow, Scotland, and was a designer, architect and water colorist who lived from June 7, 1868, to December 10, 1928. He created a style that would come to be known as Glasgow style. Napa Rose uses his style in the décor combined with the Napa Valley and California cuisine themes.

Executive Chef Andrew Sutton is a veteran of the California food scene. Tony Bruno commented, "Andrew is the perfect match to lead the Grand Napa, as he was recruited from the Auberge du Soleil in Napa Valley to be the restaurant's culinary visionary . . ." Andrew Sutton is a graduate of the prestigious Culinary Institute of America and has completed a classical French apprenticeship. He received valuable experience at two of the most luxurious hotels in Dallas: the Hotel Crescent Court and The Registry. He also spent five years at the Five-Star, Five-Diamond Award-winning Mansion on Turtle Creek and seven years as executive chef at the Ivy Award-winning Auberge du Soleil.

Napa Rose was named the best new restaurant in the 2002 Zagat dining guide survey and "Top Food" in the 2003 edition. The restaurant continues to get honors and recognition. The specialty dishes celebrate seacoast, farmlands, vineyards and ranches.

General Manager Michael Jordan is a Master Sommelier, honored by the Court of Masters. Michael is second generation to the restaurant experience and grew up in the business. He is also a favorite around the Disneyland Resort because he annually trains cast members for the Court of Masters sommelier program. He has excellent recommendations to find the perfect wine selection to accompany your meal.

This is the private entrance for guests staying a the Grand Californian Hotel.

Tim Burrows designed the pool gates. Here you see the state flower. You've heard
of Steel Magnolias? Here's an iron California Poppy.

APPENDIX A
HIDDEN MICKEY LIST

Since many people enjoy seeking out Hidden Mickeys, here is a list of them for you to locate! Each one is discussed in more detail in the book on the pages listed.

Entry or Sunshine Plaza:

In the general area of the Sunshine Plaza entry:
- Near turnstile 8, imbedded in the pavement, 20
- Near the wave pool, this Hidden Mickey is imbedded in the pavement, 29

Inside the Greetings from California Shop:
- Mickey & Minnie mural, 26
- Goofy & Pluto mural, 27
- Goofy Scuba mural, bubble, 27
- Goofy Scuba mural, in Goofy swim trunks, 27
- Mickey swim trunks, 27
- Oversized camera light bulb, 27

Hollywood Pictures Backlot:

- Elephant statues, 38
- Souvenir shop–frames, 49
- Cruella De Vil trailer, 55

Muppet Vision 3D:
- Pipes in queue
- Bombs in pre-show, 44
- Eggs in pre-show, 46
- Pre-show film, 46
- Pre-show film on Scooter's name tag, 46

- 3D film–kid holding balloon at finale, 48

Monsters Inc. attraction:
- Stars in skyline, 52
- Randall Hidden Mickey pattern, 52
- Sully (in his fur) a spot near his rump, 52

Hyperion Theater:
- Pattern over doorway, 56

Tower of Terror:
- Pre-show doll held by girl, 60
- While on elevator, the scrollwork on ghost hallway, 60

Animation Studio:
Sorcerer's Workshop:
- Gold dial sorcerer, 67
- Gold dial Mickey silhouette, 67

Beast's library:
- Fireplace screen, 70

Animation Academy:
- Deck of cards on wall, 65
- Watch wall hanging, 65
- Plushes, 65
- Rocking horse, 65
- Tambourine, 65
- Toy Mickey hanging on wall, 65
- Snow globe on desk, 65
- Bookends, 65
- Drum set, 65

Golden State:

Taste Pilots' Grill:
- Fire alarms, 77

- Engine photos, 77

Soarin':
- Pre-show kid's sweats, 79
- Pre-show Mouseketeer hat, 79
- Golf ball, 79
- Flowers at entrance of Disneyland, 80
- Mickey & Minnie characters in holiday parade, 80
- Fireworks, 80

Grizzly Recreation Area:
- Three Mickeys on entrance map, 87
- Radio call letters, 87

Bay Area:
- Sourdough bread, 92

"a bug's land":

It's Tough to Be a Bug! show:
- Lobby rock formations, 104
- Theater plants, 106

Paradise Pier:

- Treasures in Paradise store: On harness of carousel lions merchandise display, 116
- Mural at end of boardwalk, 120
- New Haul Fishery sign
- Face painting booth, 125

S.S. rustworthy:
- antennae topper, 129
- S.S. rustworthy dials, 129

Jumpin' Jellyfish:
- Bubbles on pole, 130

Mulholland Madness Mural:
- Red car with flames, registration on license plate, 132

- Another license plate as you enter attraction looking back, 132
- Swimming pool, 132

Dinosaur Jack Sunglasses Shop:
- Button collage, peaking from behind the hubcap, 133

Point Mugu:
- Display across top back wall, 133

Man Hat n' Beach:
- Octopus display, 134

Side Show Shirts:
- Man lying on bed of nails display, 134
- Betty Ducks display, 134

Grand Californian:
- Grand Californian emblem, 137
- Grandfather clock, 141
- Light fixtures and wall sconces, 143
- Portrait frame, 143
- Landscape frame, 147

New Hidden Mickeys you've discovered:

_____

_____

_____

_____

_____

_____

Please share your finds by visiting www.themeparkdetective.com and clicking on the "contact us" button. I'll include them in future editions.

APPENDIX B

TWILIGHT ZONE TELEVISION PROPS

For Twilight Zone trivia buffs, the Hollywood Tower Hotel is filled with more than 100 television props and references to the show. The Imagineers must have enjoyed their research when they reviewed every episode of *The Twilight Zone* television series. There are 156 episodes, and each episode was watched at least twice. The attraction is filled with lots of props and references to the show, and you may enjoy seeking them out. For more references, check out www.themeparkdetective.com for updates.

AS YOU ENTER THE BUILDING:

22 above the door. As you walk to the left library, notice the door on the back of the front desk office has a 22 above it. "Twenty-Two" is the name of episode 53, which aired on February 10, 1961, season two. Actor Jonathan Harris, best known from the television series *Lost in Space*, stars as the doctor. In this episode, Miss Powell has a recurring nightmare about room 22 that puts her in the hospital on the verge of a nervous breakdown. In the dream, after a sequence of repeating events, she finds herself outside room 22, the hospital's morgue, where a nurse opens the door and says, "Room for one more, honey." She screams, runs away and awakens. The next day the doctor brings the morgue nurse up to meet Miss Powell and it's not the same woman from her dream, although he is surprised that Miss Powell knows that room 22 is the morgue since she's never been there. Soon, Miss Powell recovers and is released from the hospital and is about to board a flight to Miami. She then discovers the flight is number 22 and she starts to get anxious. The sequence of events from her dream starts to repeat and with great anxiety, she climbs the stairs to board the flight. She then recognizes the flight attendant as the woman from her dream who says, "Room for one more, honey." Miss Powell refuses to step aboard and runs back to the terminal in fear. Flight 22 leaves without her and explodes during takeoff.

Thimble in cabinet at the left entrance to the library. This prop is from the 34th episode "The After Hours" that first appeared June 10, 1960, during season one. Marsha White goes to a department store to buy a gold thimble for her mother. She is taken to the ninth floor, where the only merchandise available is exactly what she wants. In returning to the ground floor she discovers that it is dented and wishes to complain. The store keepers try to tell her that there is no ninth floor. Marsha waits for assistance and falls asleep while the store closes. When she wakes up she is scared into the elevator that takes her to the ninth floor-only to realize that she is a mannequin and is only allowed to live freely for one month during the year.

Stopwatch in cabinet. This prop is from episode 124, titled, "A Kind of Stopwatch," which aired October 18, 1963, during season five. A man named McNulty meets a man named Mr. Potts in a bar. Mr. Potts gives him a stopwatch that stops time for everyone except for himself. When McNulty tries to show his friends, he finds that they are unaware of anything happening. So McNulty decides to freeze time and rob a bank. In the process, he drops his watch and is forever stuck in a timeless world.

ONCE IN THE LIBRARY: Actually, both the right and left side libraries have the same props, so don't fret which side you're assigned.

Rod Edward Serling was the creator of *The Twilight Zone* television series, which aired 156 episodes. Rod was born in Syracuse, N.Y., on December 25, 1924, and died June 28, 1975, of complications from coronary bypass surgery. *The Twilight Zone* was filmed from 1957 to 1964 and Serling wrote 92 of the episodes himself. The series won two Emmys and was a launching pad for many Hollywood stars such as Jack Klugman, Robert Redford and William Shatner. Through re-runs, the television series has become a pop culture icon for generations. The Imagineers went to great lengths to locate and acquire actual footage of Serling in the pre-show you see in the attraction.

Rod Serling Envelope. In the library, look for an envelope tucked in the bookcase that simply states "Rod Serling." The envelope is a reference to "A World of His Own," which aired July 1, 1960. In episode 36 from season one Gregory West is a married playwright.

He is quite talented in creating characters, and when he describes them onto his tape recorder they literally come to life. He appears to have a love relationship with one of his characters, Mary, and is caught by his wife holding her. When Gregory tries to explain to his wife that Mary is a fictional character, his wife decides to report him to authorities as unstable. Gregory tries to show his wife that the characters are fictional and can disappear when he cuts the tape recording and burns it in the fireplace. When his wife still doesn't believe him, he pulls out an envelope in the safe with her name on it. When she doubts him again he burns the envelope and she disappears. Gregory then re-creates Mary as his new wife. In the finale, Rod Serling begins making his closing statements and says that the situation is purely fictional and ridiculous. Then Gregory pulls out an envelope from his safe with Rod Serling's name on it. He shows the recording and scolds Rod for saying the situation was nonsensical and ridiculous and burns the envelope. Rod looks at the camera and says, "Well, that's the way it goes," and suddenly, poof, he disappears. This is the first episode of *The Twilight Zone* where Rod Serling makes an appearance.

Trumpet. Look for the trumpet in the library from the episode "A Passage for Trumpet," starring Jack Klugman. This 32nd episode aired on May 20, 1960, during season one. In this episode, out of work and down on his luck, musician Joey Crown is convinced that his life is worthless. Although he feels no one but Gabriel* plays the trumpet better, he decides to throw himself in front of a truck. When Joey wakes up he finds that he is all alone. Despondent, he goes to some of his favorite night spots, only to discover that he doesn't recognize anyone. Worse yet, no one can see or hear him. Joey then discovers that he has no reflection in the mirror. In the midst of his angst, Joey is drawn to a tall man playing a trumpet. The man addresses him, explaining that Joey is in limbo and must decide between life and death. After talking with the man, Joey chooses life, thanking him and learning his name is "Gabe." Joey then finds himself back on the pavement in front of the truck that hit him. Later that night, he goes to the rooftop and plays his trumpet, only to meet a girl that asks him to show her the town.

* In the Bible, it is Archangel Gabriel that many believe will blow a sacred trumpet horn at the Last Judgment.

Tabletop fortune-telling machine with a devil head.

In each of the libraries, on the top of the bookshelf, look for a red box with a devil head on it. The box says "Ask me a yes or no question." This is the fortune-telling machine used as a prop from the 43rd episode "Nick of Time," which aired November 18, 1960, during season two. William Shatner, famous for his role on *Star Trek,* plays newlywed Don Carter. Here, Don and his wife, Pat, wait at a cafe while their car gets repaired. The tabletop fortune-telling machine grabs Don's attention as it predicts two very vague events: a promotion at work and a near car accident. Don panics and starts feeding the machine pennies until Pat convinces him to make his own future. After they leave, another couple enters and soon becomes addicted to the machine. Rod Serling demonstrates the power of superstition.

Small Alien Spaceman.

On the top shelf, you'll see a little gold robot-looking spaceman. This prop is from the episode called "The Invaders" starring Agnes Moorehead of *Citizen Kane* and *Bewitched* fame. This 51st episode aired January 27, 1961, during season two. Moorehead plays an elderly woman who goes to the roof of her farmhouse to investigate a noise. There she finds a flying saucer with two small spacemen. She is tormented by them until she batters one of them and then destroys the spaceship with an ax. Before she kills the second creature it sends a message to its home planet not to send any more ships. When the camera focuses on the demolished saucer it reads "U.S. AIR FORCE SPACE PROBE N$^{\underline{o}}$. 1."

Reading Glasses.

In the library, under the television, you may see a pair of broken reading glasses. The glasses are from the episode called "Time Enough At Last" starring Burgess Meredith. This eighth episode aired November 20, 1959, as part of season one. Burgess Meredith plays Henry Bemis, a bank teller with a passion for reading. He longs for time to read, but his wife hates his reading and criticizes him even if he reads the bottle of ketchup. He gets in trouble with his boss at work as he tries to read there. So during lunch, he hides in the bank vault to read and a nuclear bomb destroys everything. When he emerges, he realizes that he is the only survivor. At first he is saddened until he notices that the books from the library were not harmed. He starts organizing the books, only to step on his glasses, leaving him virtually blind.

IN THE BOILER ROOM:

Chalk marks on wall. When and if your line climbs up the stairs before entering the ride elevator, you may notice a chalk rectangle drawn on the back wall with an "x" at each of the corners. This drawing represents a portal to another dimension as seen in the 91st episode "Little Girl Lost," which aired March 16, 1962, in season three. Tina is a 6-year-old girl who rolls out of bed and falls through the portal. Her parents and a neighbor can hear her but struggle to free her before the hole closes in forever. They draw a chalk line on her wall like the one you see here. Fortunately, little Tina is pulled back through the wall before the doorway closes. It is believed that this episode may have inspired the film *Poltergeist*. An episode of *The Simpsons* also makes reference to it. When and if you are near the chalk drawing, listen carefully, as you may hear little Tina crying; but be careful that you don't fall through.

As you exit the attraction, you'll be shown your photo taken at the highest point of the ride. Below the photo monitors there are several more television props, such as a toy telephone, a razor that comes to life, a camera that takes photos of the future and a typewriter.

Toy Telephone in case, below photos. This prop appeared in the 22nd episode, "Long Distance Call," which aired on March 31, 1961, in season two. Billy Bayles is a five-year-old boy who is given a toy telephone by his grandmother for his birthday. Grandma Bayles tells Billy that he can talk to her always on his phone, but she dies soon after. Billy tells his parents that grandma is on the phone and is lonely and wants him to visit her. The parents ignore his comments until he throws himself in front of a car and tells his parents he was told to do it. Late one night, the mother rushes into his bedroom, because she hears Billy talking on the phone. She picks up the receiver and hears breathing. Billy is upset that his mother may have broken his phone and runs away and tries to drown himself. A rescue team tells the parents they may be unable to revive him. The father goes to Billy's bedroom and grabs the toy telephone and pleads with his mother to let Billy grow up. At just that moment, Billy is revived.

Electric razor, radio, and typewriter with the message "Get out of here, Finchley" in cases below photos. These props relate to one episode called "A Thing About Machines." This episode aired on October 28, 1960, during season two. In this 40th episode, Bartlet Finchley is a writer who hates machines. For the last several days, his television, radio and clock have been waking him during the middle of the night. His secretary quits and the typewriter then types out on its own, "GET OUT OF HERE, FINCHLEY." The television and phone both turn on and give him the same message. His electric razor slithers down the stairs and chases him outside. Once outside, Finchley is then chased by his own car until he falls in a pool and drowns. It seems that machines hated Finchley in return.

Camera in case below photos. This prop is from season two, episode 10, called "A Most Unusual Camera," which aired December 16, 1960. Husband and wife burglars Chester and Paula Diedrich have just robbed an antique shop. One of the items they stole is a camera that takes pictures five minutes into the future. They discover this as the camera predicts the arrival of Paula's brother. They decide to take the camera to the horse races, photograph the scoreboard and use the results to win a lot of money. Back at the hotel suite, the room service waiter notices the camera has an inscription that says, "10 to an owner." The husband and brother then fight over the camera and how to use the last photos. In the struggle, both men fall out of the window. Paula takes a picture of the pavement, and the waiter returns revealing he recognizes them as criminals and demands their winnings. The camera reveals the last photo with more than two bodies on the pavement. Paula races to the window and accidentally falls out. The waiter then looks again at the photo and counts that there are actually four bodies on the ground as he falls out the window, too.

Willoughby Travel sign on the back wall away from photo screens. This refers to episode 30, called "A Stop at Willoughby," which aired May 6, 1960, in season one. Gart Williams is an unhappy man who has great pressures at work and also at home. He falls asleep on the train ride home and dreams of a town called Willoughby, circa July 1888. He dreams of Willoughby three times but doesn't get off the train until the third time-after having another bad day at work. When he decides to get off the train and stay in Willoughby, everyone is friendly and knows his name. Back in modern day, on a cold November evening, Williams is seen jumping from the train yelling something about Willoughby and is taken away in a hearse with the words Willoughby & Son Funeral Home on the door.

Can in case near entrance to store. This is a reference to episode 86 "Kick the Can," which aired February 9, 1962, season three. Charles Witley is a resident of the Sunnyvale Rest Home who believes that the secret to being young is to act young. His friend Ben Conroy adamantly disagrees. One night, Charles wakes up everyone at Sunnyvale to play kick-the-can. All agree except Ben, who instead goes to tell the superintendent, Mr. Cox. When Mr. Cox and Ben go outside all they see are children playing kick-the-can. Ben recognizes the children and asks Charles for another chance, but learns it's too late. The children run off and leave Ben to be alone.

Poster advertising the Tip Top Club. As mentioned in the Hollywood Pictures Backlot chapter, the two-hour television show that Disney created to explain the haunting of the tower was called *Tower of Terror*, which starred Steve Guttenburg and Kirsten Dunst. In their story, the name of the restaurant at the top of the hotel is the Tip Top Club.

As you exit the photo screen area, look for the Tip Top Club poster. The sign reads "The Tip Top Club proudly presents Anthony Fremont." Anthony Fremont is the primary character from episode 73 titled "It's a Good Life," which aired November 3, 1961, in season three. This episode features Bill Mumy as Anthony Fremont and Cloris Leachman as Mrs. Freemont, Anthony's mother. (Bill Mumy is also recognized as Will Robinson from the television show *Lost in Space*.) Anthony Fremont is the little boy who controls a whole town with his mind. If he thinks people have negative thoughts, he sends them away to the cornfield. Anthony decides that he doesn't like music, so no one sings. He doesn't like electricity, so people are forced to live without it. People constantly tell him how "good" things are and try to keep their thoughts "good," for fear he will destroy them. This episode is particularly important to the Twilight Zone Tower of Terror because the opening with Rod Serling was used for library footage. Serling appears in every episode of *The Twilight Zone*, and it would only be appropriate that he also appeared in the Tower of Terror, but since Serling had died years before the attraction was designed, existing footage from the 1960s and a voice double had to be used to carry on the proper intro.

The opening narration by Serling for "It's a Good Life" is the longest monologue from the series. In the television show his comments are, "Tonight's story on *The Twilight Zone* is somewhat unique and calls for a different kind of introduction. This as you may recognize is a map of the United States . . . " Of course in the Tower of Terror attraction the line reads, "This as you may recognize is a maintenance service elevator . . . " A voice actor was used to finish the line and set up the story for the attraction.

Hard-core Disney fans may point out that Bill Mumy appeared in four episodes of the television show *Disneyland*. The episodes were: *For the Love of Willadean: Treasure in the Haunted House* (1964) and *For the Love of Willadean: A Taste of Melon* (1964). He was also in *Sammy, the Way-Out Seal: Part 1* (1962) and *Sammy, the Way-Out Seal: Part 2* (1962).

APPENDIX C
SOARIN' QUEUE REFERENCES

The Soarin' Over California queue is a tribute to aviation and essentially is an air museum of "who's who" and "what's what." The photos of the significant planes and aviators all relate to California. While some of the pilots weren't born in California, you'll read about their ties to California and understand what the Imagineers found for inspiration. If you're curious, you might enjoy reading on about the influence California has had on the aviation industry.

WINGS OF FAME

The first room is a tribute to the aircraft. There are 10 banners and 18 plaques.

The banners refer to the manufacturers of the named planes.

North American P-51 Mustang

The P-51 Mustang was the first long-range fighter in World War II. From 1940-1945 North American Aviation built 15,000 planes for the British. The planes were built in Inglewood, Calif. In top production, North American was able to produce 857 planes in a single month. Prior to the P-51 Mustang entering the war, the allied forces were losing too many planes in battle against Germany. The P-51 was developed as a long-range fighter with a large gas tank holding 425 gallons. It was more economical, using half the fuel as other U.S. fighters. Its range was 1,080 miles and 2,600 miles when drop tanks were attached to the wings. This allowed the Allies to travel deep into German territory and destroy German plane manufacturing plants. The P-51's arrived in England in late 1943, early 1944. In their first battle, February 11, 1944, the Eighth Air Force command sent 49 mustangs to Oschersleben and Halberstadt. Not only did they hit their targets in both cities, but they also shot down 15 enemy planes. The P-51 was 50 mph faster than the German fighters at 28,000 feet and could out dive and out turn even though it was some 3,000 – 4,000 lbs. heavier. The P-51 Mustang inspired new air tactics that were to simply get the Germans in the air and destroy them there. Several editions of the P-51 Mustang were created using letters A-K to as upgrades were made. Models B and C added a bubble canopy and the most-produced edition was the P-51 Mustang D.

Lockheed Vega

On May 20-21, 1932 Amelia Earhart was the first woman and second person to make a non-stop solo flight across the Atlantic Ocean. Her plane was a Lockheed Vega 58 built December 4, 1928 in Burbank Calif. She bought this demonstration plane from Lockheed on March 17, 1930. Since 1966, Amelia's plane has been on display at the Smithsonian Institute.

Lockheed started plane production by building the Vega. Over the years, they built 131 of them. The Vega is known for its famous record-breaking pilots such as Amelia, but also Wiley Post, who flew his Vega 5C around the world twice. The Vega is also known for its spruce veneer monocoque (unibody) fuselage and a spruce cantilever wing. The first Vega had a top speed of 135 mph and in 1928 won every speed award at the National Air Races. The plane has a Wright Whirlwind engine which delivered 225 hp. The only thing not streamlined in the Vega was the landing gear.

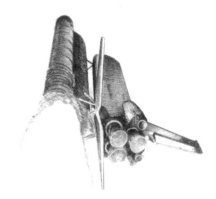

Rockwell Space Shuttle Columbia

A space shuttle is a reusable spacecraft designed to transport people and cargo to and from the Earth's orbit. National Aeronautics and Space Administration (NASA) commissioned the California based Rockwell to assemble five space shuttles; Columbia (1981), Challenger (1982), Discovery (1983), Atlantis (1985) and Endeavor (1991). The Endeavor replaced Challenger, which was destroyed in 1986 killing all seven astronauts. The Columbia was the first space shuttle to orbit the Earth. Its first flight was April 12-14, 1981, landing at Edwards Air Force Base in Southern California. A shuttle can land like a plane, but must launch attached to two rocket boosters and an external fuel tank. Rockwell International has an assembly plant in Palmdale, Calif. The Columbia was retrofitted there twice. Tragically in 2003 Columbia broke apart over Arizona and Texas as it re-entered the Earth's atmosphere killing all seven astronauts on board.

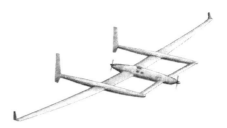

Lockheed P-38 Lightning

Lockheed, headquartered in Burbank, Calif. designed the P-38 Lightning in 1937. The P-38 was the first U.S. plane to travel more than 400 mph and named "Lightning" because it flew from California to New York flight in an unprecedented seven hours. The P-38 was nicknamed the "Fork Tail Devil" because it was the first fighter plane to have two engines in twin nacelles. It wasn't until 1942 the plane was built in any large scale. In total, 9,923 P-38 Lightning planes were built, seeing action in World War II in Europe and in the Pacific. This plane shot down more Japanese planes than any other U.S. fighter. The P-38 has a 52-foot wingspan, and is more than 32' long. The plane was designed partly by Clarence "Kelly" Johnson.

Voyager aircraft – Voyager

The Voyager was the first plane to fly around the world without stopping or refueling. The adventure took 9 days, 3 minutes and 44 seconds. The plane was piloted by Richard Rutan and Jeana Yeager. Leaving December 14, 1986 from Edwards Air Force Base, the flight became the world's longest flight. Voyager completed her journey on December 23, 1986. The plane weighs 939 lbs, but with fuel, pilots and supplies, it weighs 9,654.5 lbs. It took five years to build the plane in Mojave, Calif. and was designed by Burt Rutan (Richard's brother). The plane flew at 11,000 feet for 26,366 miles at 116 mph. This amazing venture was done without spending any federal funds, so President Ronald Reagan honored the crew with the Presidential Citizenship Medal. The first flight of Voyager was in 1983. The plane looks very futuristic with its twin rear pusher-propellers, and swept-forward wing. It has a wingspan of 110 feet 10 inches, the fuselage is 25 feet, 5 inches. The plane is equipped with a Teledyne Continental engine and is now at the Smithsonian Institute.

Douglas DC-3

Perhaps the best known aircraft in the world is the DC-3. She made her first flying debut in 1935 on the anniversary of the Wright Brothers Kitty Hawk, on December 17. Like Kitty Hawk, the flight went virtually unnoticed, yet proved to be a major milestone in aviation history. In Santa Monica, California the first DC-3 was a 14-person luxury sleeper transport built for American Airlines and was intended to transport guests from New York to Chicago non-stop. The plane had seven upper births folded into the ceiling, two dressing rooms, lavatories, a galley and even a honeymoon suite. In railroad terms the DC-3 was designed to be a flying Pullman Car. Because the fuselage was fairly wide, the DC-3 had great versatility. Quickly, more than 800 were built for commercial use, although 10,000 military versions were commissioned. In addition to Oklahoma City, Long Beach, Calif. became production sites to assist in the mass production to keep up with the military demand. The popularity of the DC-3 can be attributed to the belief that it was larger, faster, safer, more luxurious than previous planes, and economical to operate. When it celebrated its 65th anniversary there were almost 2,000 DC-3's in service.

Northrup Flying Wing

John Northrup was interested in designing and building an all-wing plane, with no tail and no identifiable body of the plane. The clean design would create a huge advantage over conventional planes because it would have very little drag. In 1923, he started designs and in 1927 he designed his first tailless plane. His plans were ahead of their time and throughout his career he would work on the Flying Wing as it would evolve. In July 1940, the first N1M "Jeep" was tested and more than 200 successful flights were made by this plane. In the 1970s the technology began to catch up with the designs and the Flying Wing would eventually be developed into the B-2 Bomber or "Stealth Bomber." The first B-2 bomber rolled out of the hangar in Palmdale, Calif. in November, 1988. This plane shares its anniversary with Disneyland; July 17, although it made its debut in 1989. The B-2 is a special plane as it can fly unobservable and can penetrate an enemy's sophisticated defenses. While many of the features regarding the stealth bomber remain classified, its coating, wing design, and composite materials allow it to fly more flexible routes and higher altitudes increasing its range and view for the aircraft sensors. If you've ever seen the B-2 bomber fly by, it makes just a whisper and you're suddenly glad that it's on OUR side.

Ryan – Spirit of St. Louis

Charles Lindbergh made the Spirit of St. Louis famous by being the first person to fly solo nonstop across the Atlantic. In 1919, Raymond Orteig, a Frenchman who owned hotels in New York, offered to pay $25,000 to anyone who could fly from Paris to New York, or New York to Paris without stopping. With a budget of $15,000, Charles Lindberg was convinced that a single-engine plane was the way to go. Although popular opinion at the time suggested three engines, Lindberg felt that three engines only tripled the risk. He wanted less weight, one pilot, one engine and was involved with almost every decision surrounding the plane. Ryan Airlines Corporation out of San Diego, Calif. offered to build the plane for $6,000 excluding the engine. The Spirit of St. Louis had a maximum range of 4,000 miles, although only 3,600 were needed for the New York to Paris flight. One of the innovative design decisions involved was placing the main fuel tank in front rather than behind the pilot's seat. For safety he didn't want to get caught between the gas tank and the engine, but the design eliminated almost any view. To see he used a periscope and a window on each side. Weight was his utmost concern, so Lindbergh flew without some major provisions such as a radio, parachute, gas gauges or navigational lights. He even designed lightweight boots for himself and replaced the leather pilot seat with a wicker chair. Departing New York Roosevelt Field, the Spirit of St. Louis flew 3,600 miles landing in Le Bourget Field in Paris in 33 1/2 hours on May 21, 1927 (Paris Time). Today, the Spirit of St. Louis plane is housed in the Smithsonian National Air and Space Museum in Washington, D.C.

LESSON TO LEARN

If you'd like to read more about Charles Lindbergh and his famous flight, pick up a copy of "The Spirit of St. Louis" by Charles A. Lindbergh.

TREASURE & TRIVIA

The first animated Mickey Mouse cartoon was *Plane Crazy*. (Although the first Mickey Mouse cartoon released in theaters was *Steamboat Willie*.) *Plane Crazy* was inspired by Charles Lindberg's famous flight. In the cartoon, Mickey even pulls back his hair in a Charles Lindbergh fashion.

North American X-15

The North American X-15 rocket-powered research aircraft served as a bridge between manned flight within the Earth's atmosphere and manned flight into space. Three of the X-15 research aircrafts were built by North American Aviation in Los Angeles, Calif. Test flights began in 1959 and the X-15 was the first winged aircraft to attain velocities of Mach 4, 5 and 6. That's four, five, and six times the speed of sound. The X-15 flew faster and higher than any other plane, with a peak altitude of 354,200 feet or about 67 miles above the Earth's surface. The plane was designed to explore the problems of flight at very high speeds and altitudes. The plane was able to withstand temperatures of 650° due to the titanium body with a covering of nickel alloy. The body was painted black to dissipate heat. The plane was launched from a modified Boeing B-52 mid-flight. The B-52 would carry the plane to 40,000 feet under a wing. The X-15 had two types of control systems: the conventional aerodynamic control systems for inside the Earth's atmosphere and special "thruster" reaction control rockets for flying on the fringes of space. The X-15 is 50'7" long, 13' high, with a wingspan of 22'4" and weighs 12,500 pounds empty. Two of the planes still exist; one is on exhibit at the Air Force Museum, Wright-Patterson Air Force Base in Ohio and another one is at the Smithsonian Institution in Washington D.C.

AeroVironment – Gossamer Condor

The Gossamer Condor is a human-powered aircraft built in 1977. The aircraft was piloted by amateur cyclist and hang-gliding pilot Bryan Allen. Allen flew the Condor for seven minutes 2.7 seconds over a closed course on August 23, 1977, winning the first Henry Kremer prize of 50,000£ ($95,000) for the first controlled human-powered flight. The Gossamer Condor was built by AeroVironment, and created by Paul B. MacCready and Dr. Peter B.S. Lissaman both of Pasadena, Calif. The Gossamer Condor was constructed of thin aluminum tubes and mylar plastic supported with a stainless steel wire. The plane is on display at the Smithsonian Institute.

HALL OF FAME
20 Banners and 22 photos

John J. Montgomery
(1858–1911)

John Joseph Montgomery was born in Yuba City, Calif, but was raised in Oakland, Calif. He ferried across San Francisco Bay to attend Santa Clara University when it was still a college. He obtained his Master's of Science Degree from St. Ignatius College. John Montgomery was an aviation pioneer, inventor, and professor of mathematics. He began experimenting with wing-flapping monoplane gliders in 1883 and made the first manned-controlled flights in the Otay Mesa area of San Diego. In 1904, a circus daredevil, Daniel J. Maloney, who parachuted from balloons, approached Montgomery about using a balloon to hoist an aeroplane to four thousand feet and gliding to the ground. The two worked together for a few months and the first flight was a 20 minute graceful descent. The second time in 1905, a dangling balloon release cable tangled above Maloney and he died in the crash. Montgomery resumed flying after mourning the loss of his friend. Montgomery died in an accident on his monoplane glider near San Jose, Calif. on October 31, 1911. He had worked with flying machines for more than 27 years and had made more than 55 successful flights at a camp at Evergreen south of San Jose. Since Montgomery didn't document his flights very well, and kept a lot of his projects secret, he hasn't been given as much credit as he probably deserves, especially considering his flights precede the Wright brothers by about 20 years. There are two historical landmarks named in his honor; one in Otay Mesa, Calif., the other in San Jose, Calif.

At least three California schools are named for him and one of the country's busiest small craft airports "Montgomery Field" in San Diego, Calif., is named for him.

LESSON TO LEARN

To read more about John Montgomery and his early days of flying gliders, check out *John Joseph Montgomery – Father of Basic Flying* by Arthur Dunning Spearman. A film titled, "Gallant Journey" by Columbia Pictures in 1946 tells his story.

Donald Wills Douglas
(1892–1981)

Donald Douglas was born in Brooklyn, N.Y. He attended the U.S. Naval Academy and in 1914 he became the first aeronautical student to earn his bachelor's degree in mechanical engineering from Massachusetts Institute of Technology (MIT). Douglas founded the Douglas Aircraft Company in 1921 in California. In 1924, he designed and produced the first airplanes to circumnavigate the Earth. His company produced civil and military aircraft including the DC-3 mentioned earlier, which has become the genesis of the modern airliner. He remained president of the company until 1957 and continued to be chairman of the board until 1967, when it merged with McDonnell Aircraft.

Chuck Yeager
(1923–)

Brigadier General Charles Elwood "Chuck" Yeager was born in Myra, W.V. He is a living legend who is a World War II flying ace and test pilot. Chuck is most famous for being the first person to travel faster than the speed of sound during a flying mission. He joined the Army in 1939 as an aircraft mechanic and was selected for flight training in 1941. In combat he flew P-51 Mustangs, "Glamorous Glennis" named for his then girlfriend, Glennis Dickhouse, who he later married. While stationed in the United Kingdom in 1944, he was shot down over France, but escaped to Spain without capture. Although there was a strict policy that no pilot who escaped should fly over enemy territory, Yeager went straight to Dwight D. Eisenhower to plead his case. He was the first pilot to make "ace in a day" when he shot down five enemy aircraft in one mission. Yeager remained in the Air Force after the war and became a test pilot. He was selected to fly the Bell X-1, a rocket-powered high-speed plane for the National Advisory Council for Aeronautics (NACA) program. NACA was the predecessor to NASA. On October 14, 1947, Chuck broke the sound barrier traveling at Mach 1 in the Bell X-1 at an altitude of 45,000 feet. The flight took off from Edwards Air Force Base in California. Interestingly, he broke two ribs while horseback

LESSON TO LEARN

In addition to reading *The Right Stuff*, Chuck Yeager's own *Yeager: An Autobiography* is recommended. You may also find his work in: *Press on! Further Adventures in the Good Life*, and *Chuck Yeager and the Bell X-1: Breaking the Sound Barrier*. Certainly Chuck Yeager is a modern hero who is uninterested in the hero business, disbelieving in the concept of "The Right Stuff."

riding just a couple of nights before the flight, but refused to tell anyone but his closest friend for fear of being pulled from the mission. Chuck Yeager has gone on to break many other speed and altitude records and a good portion of Tom Wolfe's book *The Right Stuff* talks about him. The book was also made into a film. Chuck Yeager lives in Grass Valley, Calif.

TREASURE & TRIVIA

You may want to notice the replica of the X-1 out in front of the Taste Pilots' Grill restaurant. Also in the Fly' n Buy store, the October 14, 1947 date is circled on the calendar in honor of Chuck's famous flight.

Howard Hughes
(1905 – 1976)

Howard Robard Hughes, Jr. was born in Houston Texas. It's hard to describe Howard Hughes because in his lifetime he was an engineer, aviator, industrialist, movie producer, playboy and eccentric. He never earned a diploma, but attended several fine schools, including Thacher School in Ojai, Calif. and he studied engineering at the California Institute of Technology. In spite of being head of Hughes Aircraft, he designed a number of the planes and personally set many world records with them.

On September 13, 1935, he set the world speed record of 352 mph over a test course near Santa Ana in his Hughes H-1 Racer. The H-1 Racer had a number of design innovations such as retractable landing gear, and all the rivets and joints were set flush into the body to avoid drag. The H-1 Racer was donated in 1975 to the Smithsonian and is on display. Hughes set another record by flying around the world in 91 hours in July of 1938. He shaved four days off the previous record, although he didn't fly his own plane, but a Lockheed Super Electra twin engine. He won many awards as an aviator such as the Harmon Trophy in 1936 and 1938, the Collier Trophy in 1939, and the Octave Chanute award in 1940. He also won a special congressional medal for his round-the-world flight.

Hughes also was a principal stockholder of Transcontinental and Western Air (T&WA) which later became TWA Airlines. T&WA were known for having the most advanced planes with pressurized cabins, and could fly at altitudes of 20,000 ft. Hughes realized that by flying above the turbulence, he could develop a commercial market making long distance routes available to the public.

Although his life was so diverse, he earns his wings at the Soarin' Wall of Fame most likely for his famous H-4 Hercules airplane. The U.S. government commissioned Hughes to build the H-4 Hercules, but Hughes didn't finish it until after the war. In 1947, Howard Hughes got behind the controls of the enormous flying boat proved it could fly over the water in Long Beach, Calif. This was the only time it flew and it only flew for one mile. The plane was nicknamed the "Spruce Goose" which displeased Hughes.

Hughes was one of the wealthiest people in the world and upon his death the biggest debate was who would inherit his fortune since he left no will. In 1983 the matter was finally settled and the fortune, was split between 22 cousins. He also left behind the Howard Hughes Medical Institute in Chevy Chase, Md., which was formed for the goal of basic biomedical research.

LESSON TO LEARN

You may enjoy learning more about Howard Hughes by seeing the modern film, *The Aviator* (2004) directed by Martin Scorsese and starring Leonardo DiCaprio. It also might be worth seeing the film *The Amazing Howard Hughes* from 1977 directed by William A. Graham and starring Tommy Lee Jones.

John K. "Jack" Northrop
(1895-1981)

John Knudsen Northrop was born in Newark, N.J. His family moved to Santa Barbara, Calif. in 1914. He was hired as a draftsmen in 1916 and one of the founding members of Loughead Aircraft Manufacturing Company (later Lockheed Corporation). In 1923, he joined Douglas Aircraft Company and rapidly climbed the company ladder to chief engineer. He later rejoined Loughead, (renamed Lockheed) and worked on the Lockheed Vega the plane used by Amelia Earhart.

In 1932, he founded the first Northrop Corporation backed by Donald Douglas in El Segundo, Calif. The company built two highly successful monoplanes: the Northrop Gamma and the Northrop Delta, which made significant improvements in flight performance and airframe life.

By 1939 he struck out on his own, leaving the old Northrop Corporation to a division of Douglas and founded a new independent company Northrop Aircraft Inc. in Hawthorne, Calif. There he served as President, Head of Engineering, and Chief of Research and concentrated on developing his flying wing design. He produced at least four separate flying wing designs: the Northrop N-1M, Northrop N-9M, Northrop YB-35, and Northrop YB-49. The flying wing could carry any weight faster, farther and cheaper than conventional aircraft. During WWII years he developed the Black Widow, the first American night interceptor, of which 700 were constructed and performed well.

Northrop retired in 1952, possibly because the defense industry was downsizing and stockholder expectations were increasing. The company had a long list of managers, but in 1980 Thomas V. Jones was the chief executive officer and invited Jack Northrop to come in for a secret meeting. When he arrived, a box was brought out and opened so he could see the "Advanced Technology Bomber" or ATB. Jack Northrop seemed pleased and with tears in his eyes said, "Now I know why God has kept me alive for the last 25 years." The ATB had no propeller shafts and housings like his YB-35, there were no fins like the YB-49. The following year Jack Northrop died at the age of 85.

In 1972, he was named into the International Aerospace Hall of Fame and the Aviation Hall of Fame in 1974. In Lancaster, Calif., there is an elementary school named after him.

Jimmy Doolittle
(1896-1993)

James Harold "Jimmy" Doolittle was born in Alameda, Calif., and spent a great deal of his youth in Nome, Alaska. He attended Los Angeles Junior College before enlisting as a flying cadet in the Signal Corps Reserve in October of 1917. During the war he stayed in the United States and worked as a flight instructor. Between World War I and World War II, Doolittle became one of the most famous pilots of his time. He made many pioneering flights cross-country, flying including one from Pablo Beach, Fla., to San Diego, Calif., in less than 22 hours. The U.S. Army gave him a Distinguished Flying Cross for this experience. Although he never finished his studies, as he left school to serve in World War I, he was awarded his bachelor's degree from the University of California at Berkeley in 1922. In 1923, after serving as a test pilot and aeronautical engineer he entered Massachusetts Institute of Technology (MIT). The military gave him two years to earn his degree, but he finished in one and earned a second Distinguished Flying Cross for his thesis on aircraft acceleration. With his extra year to school, he went on to earn his Sc.D. or "Doctor of Science" degree in aeronatics. His most important contribution to aeronautical technology was the development of instrument flying. In 1929, he was the first pilot to take off, fly, and land using only his instruments. He helped develop the artificial horizon and directional gyroscope. During the 1930s, he continued to set records, win races, and consult Shell Oil Company to produce aviation gasoline. But it was World War II that launched Doolittle into timeless notoriety with a project called Doolittle's Raid.

Doolittle returned to active military service in 1940. He was promoted to Lieutenant Colonel in 1942 and went to Headquarters of the Army Air Forces to plan an aerial raid on the Japanese. The attack included 16 B-25 bombers from the USS Hornet, with targets in Tokyo, Kobe, Osaka, and Nagoya. It was his first and only combat mission of his military career. The one-way mission took place on April 18, 1942, and it gave

America hope following the attack on Pearl Harbor. Many of the fliers died on the mission, but Doolittle bailed out of his plane and landed in a heap of manure in a rice paddy in China near Chu Cow. He was helped by Chinese guerillas to return to the United States. Although the raid caused very little damage, it demonstrated that the Japanese homeland was vulnerable and forced them to withdraw several front-line fighter units to protect it.

LESSON TO LEARN

There are two films that portray Doolittle's Raid; *Thirty Seconds Over Tokyo* (1944) starring Spencer Tracy as Doolittle, and *Pearl Harbor* (2001) with Alec Baldwin as Lt. Col. Doolittle.

Jimmy Doolittle was promoted to Lieutenant General in 1944. In 1946 he reverted to inactive status and served as vice president of Shell Oil, and was the first president of the U.S. Air Force Association in 1947. In 1951, he was appointed to Air Force chief of staff and he retired from the Air Force in 1959. The U.S. Congress promoted Doolittle to General on the Air Force retired list in 1985 and President Reagan pinned on his four-star insignia.

For the Tokyo raid, he was honored with a Medal of Honor, but during his career he received Two Distinguished Service Medals, The Silver Star, the Bronze Star, four Air Medals and decorations from Great Britain, France, Belgium, China and Ecuador. He died in California and is buried at Arlington National Cemetery near Washington DC.

Glenn L. Martin
(1886-1955)

Glenn Luther Martin was born in Macksburg, Iowa. His family moved to Southern California in 1905 where he became a young entrepreneur. At the age of 22 he owned Ford and Maxwell car dealerships in Santa Ana, Calif. He worked with his auto mechanics in a church building to build his first planes. What he lacked in technical training he had in business sense. In 1909, he taught himself to fly and he quickly set records for altitude, speed and endurance. By 1911, he was considered one of the most famous "pioneer birdmen."

He set out to be a manufacturer of biplanes and named his company Glenn L. Martin Aircraft Company. He started by building military trainers in Santa Ana, Calif., in 1912, and by 1916 he accepted a merger with the Wright Company renaming it to Wright-Martin Aircraft Company. The venture did not go well so Martin left and started another Glenn L. Martin company in September 1917 based in Cleveland, Ohio. Martin had an interest for large planes and was primarily known for bombers, seaplanes and military contracts. His first success was the MB-1 Bomber ordered by the U.S. Army in 1918. The MB-1 was too late for World War I. During four decades Glenn Martin was the senior aircraft manufacturer in the United States and the Martin Company remained under his direct control. The company built more than 11,000 planes before it ceased aircraft production in 1960. The company diversified to producing missiles, space hardware, guidance systems, sonar and avionics until its merger with Lockheed in 1995. Martin had an eye for talent and had some of the most famous and talented people working for him. They later struck out on their own, including William Boeing, Donald Douglas, Lawrence Bell, and James S. McDonnell. He was inducted in the International Aerospace Hall of Fame in 1977 posthumously. He has an airport, an aviation museum and a wind tunnel in Maryland named for him.

Jacqueline Jackie Cochran
(1906 – 1980)

Bessie Lee "Jackie" Pittman was born in Muscogee, Fla. She married Jack Cochran, had a son, and worked as a beautician. Her life began to change after her husband died, and her son was later lost in a fire. She moved to New York City in 1929 and got a job at a fashionable salon at Saks Fifth Avenue with the dream of starting her own line of cosmetics. While traveling with her clients she met millionaire Floyd Bostwick Odlum, who would be her biggest supporter and future husband. She shared her dream of a cosmetic line and the need to learn to fly to sell the cosmetics across the country. Odlum suggested she learn to fly and in 1932 she earned her pilot's license. Cochran polished her flying skills at a California flight school and competed in her first race in 1934. Approximately 1935, she moved to Indio, Calif., outside Palm Springs. In 1937 and 1938, she began to win races and set records. She flew from New York to Miami in 4 hours, 12 minutes and 27 seconds and achieved a new women's national speed record of 203 mph. She received the most outstanding pilot of the year Clifford Harmon Trophy. In March of 1939, she set a women's national altitude record at 30,052 feet, and then set two new world records for fastest times over the 1,000 and 2,000 kilometer courses.

In World War II, she became a Wing Commander in the British Auxiliary Transport Service. When the U.S. entered the war she offered her services to the Army Air corps and formed the Women's Air Force Service Pilots (WASPs) that would ferry U.S.-built bombers to England. Here she was the first civilian to be awarded the U.S. Distinguished Service Medal.

After the war she continued to race and set records. In the early 1950s she was the first woman to break the sound barrier. In the 1960s she worked as a test pilot for Northrop and Lockheed where her record was 1,429 mph, the fastest a woman has ever flown. In the 1970s she slowed down due to a serious heart condition. She received a lot of awards and recognition for her outstanding aviation career. Incidentally, she also excelled in her cosmetic business that she continued to run. The Associated Press named her "Woman of the Year" for two consecutive years in the 1950's. Jackie Cochran has earned more than 200 awards and trophies, had consulted for the U.S. Air Force, the FAA and the National Aeronautics and Space Administration and served on boards for museums and nonprofit organizations. She died in Indio, Calif., leaving a legacy and role model for future generations.

LESSON TO LEARN

Jackie's sister Billie Pittman Ayers wrote a biography about Jacqueline Cochran titled *Superwoman Jacqueline Cochran: Family Memories about the Famous Pilot, Patriot, Wife and Business Woman.*

TREASURE & TRIVIA

The U.S. Post office honored Jacqueline Cochran with a 50 cent stamp in 1997.

Florence Lowe "Pancho" Barnes
(1901 – 1975)

Florence Leontine Lowe was born to a wealthy family in San Marino, Calif., and was expected to be a society lady. She was however, a bit of a tomboy and enjoyed fishing, camping, hunting and horseback riding. Her grandfather had established the Union Army Balloon Corps during the American Civil War, so her aviation ambition was well rooted. Her mother's effort to settle her down led to her marriage in 1919 with Reverend C. Rankin Barnes, with whom she had a son.

In 1924, her mother passed away and in 1928 she inherited the family fortune. During this period she was tired of the peaceful life and abandoned her family. She disguised herself as a man and stowed away on a freighter headed to Mexico. Once in Mexico she jumped ship with another crew member and traveled around Mexico by donkey. She was given the nickname "Pancho" erroneously after the character Sancho Panza from novel *Don Quixote*. By 1941 her marriage ended in divorce.

After spending four months in Mexico, Pancho returned to San Marino. As she was taking her cousin to flying lessons, she decided to learn to fly, and after only six hours of training she soloed. She sometimes would fly over her ex-husband's Sunday morning congregation. She was one of only 24 female pilots. She then ran a barn-storming show, competed in air races and broke Amelia Earharts' world speed record of 196 mph. She moved to Hollywood and worked as a stunt pilot, including Howard Hughes' 1930 epic *Hell's Angels*. The Great Depression and family disputes drained her fortune, so in 1935 she left Hollywood, sold her apartment and bought 80 acres of land in the Mojave Desert. (This area is now annexed into Edwards Air Force Base.)

In the desert she built the Happy Bottom Riding club, also known as the Rancho Oro Verde Fly-Inn Dude Ranch. She catered to the pilots in the nearby Muroc Field. The rancho earned international fame and is where she met and became friends with many early test pilots such as Chuck Yeager, Jimmy Doolittle, and Buzz Aldrin. Pancho's ranch was famous for its parties and high-flying lifestyles. However, in 1952 she had a conflict with the U.S. Air Force which led to her eviction. The next year a suspicious fire burned down the ranch. Pancho filed a lawsuit against the U.S. Air Force stating that "My grandfather founded the United States Air Force" and the court found in her favor and reinstated her property and $375,000. She returned to the base and was referred to as "the Mother of Edwards AFB." The officer's mess was renamed the Pancho Barnes Room. She died of a heart attack in 1975.

TREASURE & TRIVIA

In Tom Wolfe's best-selling novel and 1983 film *The Right Stuff* you get a glimpse of Pancho's personality and lifestyle.

Frederick "Fred" J. Wiseman
(1875-1961)

Fred Wiseman was born in Santa Rosa, Calif. In 1909, he was a successful automobile racing driver, but his interests soon turned to aviation. In 1910, he built the first airplane in California. Inspired by designs from Wright, Curtiss, and Farman, his biplane had forward and rear elevators and ailerons on both the upper and lower wings. The plane was built near San Francisco and weighed 670 lbs, with a 50 hp engine. With the second version of his plane he started to win honors. He took second place overall in the novel class at a meet in San Francisco. In that event he won the distance event, made the longest sustained flight (6 minutes) and took the prize for most air time of 49 minutes and 43 seconds. His performance gave him national recognition. This airplane is in the National Air and Space Museum in Washington, D.C.

Wiseman is given credit for the first airplane-carried mail flight sanctioned by the U.S. Post office. He was returning home after an air-show and carried 50 copies of the Santa Rosa's local newspaper, a sack of coffee beans and three letters documenting his trip. On February 17, 1911, he was given the letters, but it took him two days to travel what should have been a 12 1/2 minute trip over 18 miles from Petaluma to Santa Rosa, Calif. Although it was sanctioned by a local post office, it precedes a flight by Earle Ovington on September 23, 1911, where mail was carried from Garden City, Long Island to Mineola.

James Herman Banning
(1899-1933)

James Banning was born in Oklahoma. He had a boyhood dream to be a pilot, but African-Americans at that had difficulty getting into flight school. He studied electrical engineering at Iowa State College for just over a year, then he was able to learn how to pilot a plane at Raymond Fisher's Flying Field in Des Moines, Iowa. He was the first black aviator to get a pilot's license from the U.S. Department of Commerce. From 1922-1928 he operated the J.H. Banning auto Repair Shop in Ames, Iowa. He left Ames in 1929 to be the chief pilot for Bessie Coleman Aero Club in Los Angeles, Calif. There he became a demonstration pilot flying a biplane named "Miss Ames." In 1932, he and another black pilot and mechanic Thomas C. Allen became the first black aviators to fly coast-to-coast. Because they flew in an old biplane pieced together from junkyard parts and because they had to raise money every time they landed to take off again, they were affectionately called the "Flying Hobos." The 3,300 mile trip from Los Angeles to Long Island required 21 days to complete because of their need to do fundraising activities. The airtime was 41 hours and 27 minutes.

 LESSON TO LEARN

To learn more about black aviators, pick up a copy of *African-American Aviators* by Stanley P. Jones. It includes short biographies of James Herman Banning as well as Bessie Coleman, William J. Powell, Benjamin O. Davis Jr., and General Daniel James Jr.

Banning died in an air show plane crash in San Diego in 1933. He was the passenger in a biplane that stalled and entered into an unrecoverable spin.

Hundreds of spectators witnessed the crash. The resourceful skills and perseverance of James Banning earned him his honor here on the walls of Soarin'.

Alys Harrison McKey (Tiny) Bryant
(1880-1954)

Alys McKey was born in Lauramie Township, Ind. She became a famed aviator and also a submarine diver. She learned to fly in 1912 in Los Angeles, taught by her future husband when she answered an ad that read, "Wanted; young lady to learn to fly for exhibition purposes." She once set a U.S. altitude record for women of 2,900 feet. Alys was the first woman to fly in Washington, Idaho, Oregon and Canada. The Canadian title won her the honor on the Soarin' wall, on July 31, 1913, where she flew for the Prince of Wales and Duke of York. Eight days later, she witnessed the death of her pilot husband Johnny Bryant, in an air show at Victoria, British Columbia. She retired from flying after her husband's death. For a short time she took to the skies again to fly for a movie filmed in Seattle, but then she retired from the skies.

Amelia Earhart
(1897-1937)

Amelia Earhart was born in Atchison, Kan. Many years later at the Kansas State Fair in Atchison she would have her first introduction to aviation. She began her career in 1921 in Los Angeles when she took flying lessons and bought her first plane. She faced some financial difficulty and sold the plane in 1924 and worked as a social worker until she received a phone call in 1928 that asked if she'd like to "fly the Atlantic?" No one had every flown over

of the Atlantic Ocean before so this was a great opportunity. She was asked to join pilot Wilmer "Bill" Stultz and co-pilot Louis E. "Slim" Gordon as they left Trepassey Harbor, NewFoundland, on June 17, 1928 and arrived in Burry Port, Wales, 21 hours later. From that adventure forward she never looked back and made flying her life. She met her future husband, book publisher and publicist George P. Putnam in preparing for the Atlantic crossing. She came home to a ticker-tape parade and the support of a country. From then on she had many records to set, and "firsts" in flying to achieve. Perhaps her most famous flight was to be her last. In 1937, she made an effort to circumnavigate the globe, but the first to use a chosen route. She disappeared during this flight and was never heard from again. The United States government spent $4 million dollars looking for Amelia. The tragic and mystery surrounding her death has inspired many writers. Theories ensued from ditching in sea, kidnapped by the Japanese, anonymously returning to the U.S. to quietly live out her life, to being captured by UFOs.

Allan Lockheed
(1889 – 1969)

Allan Haines Laughead a.k.a. Loughead was born in Niles, Calif. His father was a truck gardener and farmer and his mother was a writer. He and his brother Malcolm attended public school and didn't have many of the advantages one would think of for an aeronautical engineer and airplane manufacturing executive. Mid 1910, Allan moved to Chicago and entered into the aviation business as a mechanic for a Montgomery glider and Glenn Curtiss pusher biplane. He taught himself to fly later that same year. He became a daredevil after that and gave airplane shows for almost nothing. By 1916, Laughead moved back to California and established the Loughead Aircraft Manufacturing Company with his brother in a garage near the water front in Santa Barbara. Funded by a Santa Barbara businessman who was interested in aviation, they hired engineer John K. Northrop who would later found his own aircraft firm. Most of the designs were Northrop's, as both Laughead brothers were self-taught. They created the F-1 Seaplane, the world's largest sea-plane but with only modest success. They had better success with a S-1 single engine monocoque bi-plane, and it earned great endorsements, but World War I was over and there wasn't a great need for the plane. The business went under by 1921 and the brothers went separate ways. By late 1926, Malcolm changed his name to Lockheed so that other people could pronounce it correctly. He reunited with his brother and they re-entered the aviation business. Moving to Hollywood, the Lockheed Aircraft Company designed and built the Vega. This would be the plane that Amelia Earhart flew on her non-stop flight across the Atlantic. Allan sold the company to Detroit Aircraft Corporation in 1928 and the company went bankrupt during the depression. In 1932, a financial investor purchased the company, saved the name and continued to develop innovative planes such as the Electra, Constellation, and P-38 Lightning. Allan legally changed his name to Lockheed in 1934 and he went on to form two other aircraft manufacturing companies, both unsuccessfully. He served as an aviation consultant and an informal relationship with the Lockheed Air Corporation until his death in 1969. Lockheed Corporation merged with Martin Marietta to form Lockheed Martin and continues to develop airliners, fighters, military transports, patrol and reconnaissance machines, helicopters, missiles and space technology.

Evelyn "Bobbi" Trout
(1906–2003)

Evelyn, "Bobbi" Trout was born in Greenup, Ill. She got her nickname from her haircut ala screen star Irene Castle, and the name stuck. She learned to fly in 1928 at Burdett Air Lines, Inc., School of Aviation in Los Angeles and was the fifth women in the U.S.A. to get her transport license, number 2613. She set a solo endurance record for women by flying 12 hours and 11 minutes. But when Elinor Smith beat her record less than a month later, she took to the skies and flew 17 hours and 24 minutes. She wanted to fly longer, but the plane started to cut out as she was running out of fuel. Four months after that she climbed into a Golden Eagle Chief and flew to 15,200 feet and beat an altitude record for light class aircraft. Soon after, Will Rogers named a women's transcontinental race the "Powder Puff Derby" and Bobbi wanted to be a part of it. She jumped into the Golden Eagle Chief and started the race from Santa Monica to Cleveland. Twice she had engine troubles, but managed to make "dead-stick" landings. She knew she wasn't going to win, but she completed the race. Shortly after that, several of the women pilots created a women's flying organization and Bobbi was one of the founders of the "Ninety-Nines." Bobbi then partnered with Elinor Smith and flew the first women's in-flight fueling operation. The women stayed aboard for 42 hours and five minutes breaking a new record. Bobbi became an instructor pilot, an Aero

Police Woman, captain of the Women's Air Reserve, a Civil Air Patrol during World War II and director of the Aviation Archives in California. She continued her love of aviation, and in 1974 she was awarded the OX5 Pioneer Woman of the Year Award. In 1984, she was inducted into the OX5 Aviation Pioneers Hall of Fame.

TREASURE & TRIVIA

Lt. Col. Eileen Collins took Bobbi's pilot license into space when Eileen became the first woman pilot of the shuttle.

William J. Powell
(1899-1942)

William J. Powell was born in Henderson, Ky., and raised in Chicago. During his college years at the University of Illinois he decided to serve in World War I as an infantry lieutenant. He was badly wounded in a gas attack and went back to Illinois to finish his degree in electrical engineering. In 1934, he wrote a fictional autobiography *Black Wings*. The book talks about how he visited Le Bourget Airfield soon after Lindbergh landed there, and took his first airplane ride. He talks about being rejected by a flying school in the Army Air Corps, but received flying lessons in Los Angeles in 1928. When Powell got his pilot license in 1932, he was also licensed as a navigator and aeronautical engineer. He founded the Bessie Coleman Aero Club, named for the first black woman to fly. Bessie Coleman was a stunt pilot who died in an air show in 1926. Powell also organized an all-Negro air show in Los Angeles and attracted 15,000 people. Powell built his own flying school and

shop. He died in 1942 by what is believed to be a result of the poison gas from his World War I accident. William J. Powell is well known for urging blacks to acquire the skills to become pilots, mechanics and aviation business leaders. He inspired blacks to breakdown the barriers of racism by attaining economic power in the air.

LESSON TO LEARN

To learn more about William J. Powell, pick up a copy of *Black Wings*. Another source titled *African-American Aviators* includes stories about Bessie Coleman, William J. Powell, James Herman Banning among others.

LESSON TO LEARN

To learn more about Bessie Coleman pick up a copy of *Fly High! The Story of Bessie Coleman* by Louise Bordon. Another source that is worth reading is *Bessie Coleman: First Black Woman Pilot* by Connie Plantz.

Paul B. MacCready
(1925 -)

Paul MacCready was born in New Haven, Conn. In his youth, he was a serious model airplane enthusiast and set many records for experimental craft. At age 16, he soloed in powered planes, and in World War II he flew for the U.S. Navy. He graduated from Hopkins School in 1943, and in 1947 he received his bachelor's in physics from Yale University, where his interest in flight began to include piloting glides.

He won the 1948, 1949 and 1953 U.S. National Soaring Championships and pioneered high altitude wave soaring. During 1946 and 1956, he worked on sailplane development, soaring techniques, meteorology, and invented the Speed Ring Airspeed Selector, which is used by glider pilots to select the best flight speed between thermals. This glider speed depending on the glider's rate of sink at different air speeds is called the "MacCready Theory" or the "MacCready Speed." In 1948, he earned a Ph.D. in aeronautics from the California Institute of Technology. He founded Meteorology Research Inc., a firm in weather modification and atmospheric science research. In 1971, he started AeroVironment Inc. headquartered in Monrovia, Calif. The company develops and produces Unmanned Aerial Vehicle Systems and Energy Technologies in the fields of alternative energy, power electronics and energy efficient vehicles for operation on land, in the air or in the water. In 1977, MacCready found international fame when he made the first sustained, controlled flight in his Gossamer Condor, a 70 pound aircraft, that is powered solely by his muscles. For this he won the $95,000 Henry Kremer Prize and two years later his team created the Gossamer Albatross, another 70-pound craft with a 96-foot wingspan that flew across the English Channel. Although he wasn't the pilot, the group won another Kremer prize of $213,000. The largest cash prize in aviation at its time. He created the Condor's successors: the Gossamer Penguin and the Solar Challenger, and was involved in the development of solar-powered flying wings such as the Helios, and a solar-powered car called the Sunraycer. He continues to study battery-powered and alternative-fuel vehicles. He has

five honorary degrees, written many articles and authored and co-authored over 100 formal reports in the field of aeronautics, soaring, and ultra light craft. He is on the lecture circuit talking about creativity and development of broad thinking skills. He currently lives in Pasadena, Calif., with his wife.

LESSON TO LEARN

When you get a chance, read his biography *More with Less: Paul MacCready and the Dream of Efficient Flight* by Paul Ciotti.

T. Claude Ryan
(1898 – 1982)

Tubal Claude Ryan was an aviator and industrialist who was born in Parsons, Kan. He learned to fly in 1921 at the Air Service Flight School at March Field in California. He founded the Ryan Flying Company in 1922 in San Diego and created the first-year round passenger service; (San Diego to Los Angeles). Ryan is best known for building Charles Lindbergh's plane *Spirit of St. Louis.* He founded the Ryan Aeronautical Company which built the popular Ryan Sport Trainer (Ryan ST). The Ryan ST was a low-wing tandem-seat monoplane. The Ryan ST, and subsequent Ryan STA Special and STM eventually evolved to the PT -16, PT-20, PT-21 and PT-22 planes that the U.S. Army Air Corps ordered for pilot training. He also established the Ryan School of Aeronautics which trained some 22,000 pilots during World War II. After the war, the company diversified, to missiles, unmanned aircraft fields and experimental research aircraft. In 1968, the Company was acquired by Teledyne for $128 million and Ryan retired as chairman in 1969. In 1999, the company was eventually sold to Northrop Grumman.

Elbert L. "Burt" Rutan
(1943 –)

Elbert Leander "Burt" Rutan was born in Portland, Oregon. In 1965 he graduated third in his class from California Polytechnic University with a aeronautical engineering degree. From 1965-1972 he worked for the U.S. Air Force at Edwards Air Force Base as a flight test project engineer. In 1974, he struck out on his own and created the Rutan Aircraft Factory in the Mojave Desert. He has designed hundreds of aircraft, but is most famous for his design of the record-breaking Voyager. In 2004, he made headlines again with his SpaceShipOne, which was the first private craft which was privately funded to reach space twice in the same year, winning the Ansari "X Prize". Virgin Galactic, an off-shoot of Virgin Airlines, announced that it will begin space tourism flights in 2008 using SpaceShipTwo.

LESSON TO LEARN

The Ansari X Prize was a $10,000,000 reward for the first non-governmental, reusable, manned spacecraft. The spacecraft had to carry at least three crew members, reach an altitude of 328,000' twice within two weeks. Only 10 percent of the craft was allowed to be replaced in the relaunch. Twenty-six teams from around the world participated. Rutan's SpaceShipOne made its first flight on September 29, 2004 and won the prize on October 4, 2004, the anniversary of Sputnik. The XPrize is significant because it opens the door for the pubic to travel in space.

Clarence L "Kelly" Johnson
(1910-1990)

Kelly Johnson was born in Ishpeming, Mich. He earned his Master's Degree in aeronautical engineering and joined Lockeed in 1933. At the age of 29, he single-handedly designed the Hudson Bomber. Kelly also designed the F-80, America's first production jet, the double sonic F-104; the high altitude U-2 and the SR-71. In 1952, he was named Lockheed's chief engineer. In 1958, he was named vice president and in 1964 a member of the board of directors. He served the company for almost 50 years, designing more than 40 world-renowned aircraft. He was honored with the Medal of Freedom in 1964 by President Lyndon B. Johnson and the National Security Medal by Ronald Reagan in 1983. Kelly mentioned to Reagan that the two Californians were neighbors as both had ranches in Santa Barbara County. "But, there's a difference in the two ranches," Reagan teased. "Yours has heat."

Katherine Cheung
(1904 - 2005)

Katherine Sui Fun Cheung was born in Canton, China. In Cantonese Sui Fun means "long life" and "courage." At the age of 17 she left China and her family to study music at the Los Angeles Conservatory of Music. She left school and married George B. Young, her father's business partner and with his support, she kept her name. In 1932, her father took her for a flying lesson at Dycer Airfield in Gardena, Calif. Shortly after that, she was the first Chinese woman in U.S. History to be licensed to fly a plane. In 1935, she obtained an international license and flew as a commercial pilot, crop dusting. She rather enjoyed barrel rolls, inverted flying, loop-de-loops and other stunt flying and earned money that way. The Ninety Nines Club for women invited her to join and Amelia Earhart became a good friend. She never won speed records or set altitude or endurance records, although she regularly entered races. She participated in the Powder Puff Derby in her Ryan ST biplane that was purchased for her by the Chinese community and actress Anna May Wong for $2,000 in 1934. On her way home from the Derby, she had a close call when she discovered her compass was broken. She was also without a radio and she was forced to navigate herself to an opening through a thicket of trees. The experience scared her when stunt flying had not. After Japan invaded China she returned to China giving speeches in large Chinese communities to inspire people to learn to fly. She got the idea to start a women's aviation school in China and was collecting funds when she heard of Earhart's disappearance. She was grief-stricken and tried to bring up her morale by focusing on flying. As her cousin was presenting her with a new Ryan ST plane and tried to pull a prank fly by. He hopped into the plane, took-off and moments later crashed, killing himself for all to see. Soon after, when her father was on his deathbed, her father asked her not to fly, which she agreed to. Shortly after her father's death, she couldn't help herself and took to the skies again for a short while. At the age of 38, she hung up her wings. In spite of her grief, and loss of her dream school, she continued to inspire others. She died in California after celebrating her 100th birthday. The Smithsonian National Air and Space Museum recognizes her as the nation's first Asian aviatrix. Carol Nye created a billboard in Metro Plaza Chinatown, Los Angeles, with her picture on it.

Robert L. "Bob" Cardenas
(1920-)

Bob Cardenas was born in Merida, Yucatan, Mexico, but moved to San Diego, Calif. when he was five years old. He attended San Diego State University and in 1939 he joined the California National Guard, where he served a long and distinguished military career. He entered into aviation cadet training in 1940 and received his pilot wings in 1941. He was sent to Kelly Field, Texas, to become a flight instructor, and then to Twentynine Palms, Calif. to establish the U.S. Army Airforce's glider training school. Cardenas soon became a flight test officer, and then the director of flight test unit at Wright Field, Ohio.

His next assignment was to join the 44th Bomb Group (known as the Flying 8-balls), and in January 1944 he was sent to England and flew his first mission, a B-24H called "Southern Comfort." During his 20th mission just two months later, while flying over Germany, he and his aircraft were badly damaged by enemy fighters. He continued his mission targeting the Manzell Air Armaments plant in Freidrichshafen, Germany. Afterward he was forced to bail out of the plane as it would not make the return. The plane crashed in Fehraltdorf, Switzerland, and Cardenas landed on the shore of Lake Constance on the German side. He swam to the Swiss shore of the lake and contacted the local resistance, where he made his way to France and then back to England.

He returned to the U.S. and was assigned to the Flight Test Division once again, testing more bomber planes. In 1947, Cardenas was selected as the officer in charge of the X-1 project with Capt. Chuck Yeager as the pilot. Cardenas was the pilot of the B-29 launch craft, which had its own risks. Cardenas was the B-29 pilot on all of Yeager's flights. On one flight, the X-1 refused to release from the shackle mechanism and Cardenas had to land the B-29 with the X-1 still attached, and Yeager was unable to fully empty the fuel. The landing was nearly a three-point and the X-1 was saved from damage. Shortly after that, Yeager made his famous flight breaking the sound barrier, with Cardenas piloting the B-29.

In 1947, Cardenas made his first flight in the Northrop YB-49 "Flying Wing." About when the phase II evaluation tests were complete, he was given the opportunity to finish his Engineering degree at University of Southern California. Captain Glen Edwards replaced Cardenas and Cardenas first set off to Dayton, Ohio, to marry his sweetheart Gladys. While driving to introduce his bride to his family he heard on the radio that the Flying Wing had crashed and Captain Glen Edwards among others were killed. Cardenas school orders were cancelled and he was asked to return and finish testing the Flying Wing and search out the cause of the crash.

On February 9th, 1949, Cardenas flew non-stop from Muroc to Andrews Air Force Base, setting a new transcontinental record in four hours and five minutes. Cardenas continued to test fighters and bombers until 1955. In 1968, he was promoted to Brigadier General and in 1973 he retired from the USAF. He was honored by the Distinguished Service Medal Legion of Merit with Oak Leaf Cluster, Distinguished Flying Cross, Purple Heart, meritorious Service Medal, Air Medal with four Oak Leaf Clusters and given the Presidential Citation. He worked in private industry from 1973-1983 until he was appointed to the White House as the California Coordinator for President Reagan's Southwest Border Economic Action Group. He resigned in 1985 and continues to serve on advisory boards and chairmen of many noteworthy organizations. He is a living legend who enjoys life in San Diego with his wife Gladys and their children and grandchildren.

APPENDIX D

FAMOUS BUILDINGS REFERENCES IN HOLLYWOOD PICTURES BACKLOT

Many people enjoy looking at the different kinds of architectural styles California has to offer. The façades in the Hollywood Pictures Backlot have amusing names and bear a striking resemblance to famous landmarks found in Los Angeles.

○ LESSON TO LEARN

The Hollywood Heritage Inc. has a 90-minute walking tour of Hollywood every Sunday morning. The tour is limited to 10 people, costs $10 for non-members and begins at 9a.m. Reservations are required, but if you'd like to enjoy some of the historical Hollywood represented in DCA it would be worth it to take the tour. Reservations can be made at (323) 465-6716 or check out their website at www.hollywood heritage.org.

Below is a chart that will give you the Disney version of the building, referenced to the historical building, the year it was built, the name of the architect and the address should you want to create your own Hollywood architectural tour based on the inspiration of DCA.

DCA Building	Building in Los Angeles/ year built/architect	Address of historic building in Los Angeles
Greetings from California Spire	**Crossroads of the World** Year built: 1936 Architect: Robert V. Derrah	6671 Sunset Blvd.
The Beverly	**Wiltern Theater** Year built: 1931 Architect: Stiles O. Clements	3780 Wilshire Blvd.

Hollywood Tower Hotel	**Hollywood Roosevelt Hotel** Year built: 1927/1929 Architect: unknown	7000 Hollywood Blvd.
	Los Angeles City Hall Year built: 1928 Architect:s Albert C. Martin Sr., John Parkinson, Donald Parkinson, John C. Austin	200 N. Spring St.
	Pantages/Warner Year built: 1920 Architect: B. Marcus Priteca	401 W. 7th St.
	INTERIOR: **Biltmore Hotel** Year built: 1923 Architects: Schultze & Weaver	506 S. Grand Ave.
Hyperion Theater	**Los Angeles Theater** Year built: 1930 - 1931 Architect: S. Charles Lee	615 S. Broadway
*Coca-Cola Stand	**Mel's Drive-In** Year built: 1947 Architect: unknown * In San Francisco, not L.A.	Demolished in 1972
Argyle Building	**Argyle Hotel** Year built: 1929 Architect: Leland A. Bryant	8358 Sunset Blvd.
Role Models	**Max Factor Make-Up Studio** Year built: 1931 Architect: S. Charles Lee	1660 N. Highland Ave.

Pantages Theater (in mural)	**Pantages Theater** Year built: 1929 Architect: B. Marcus Priteca	6233 Hollywood Blvd.
Award Wieners/ back building	**Bullock's Wilshire** Year built: 1929 Architects: John & Donald B. Parkinson	3050 Wilshire Blvd.
El Capitan Theater (in mural)	**El Capitan Theater** Year built: 1925 Architects: Morgan, Walls and Clements	6838 Hollywood Blvd.
Restrooms	**Storer Residence** Year built: 1923 Architect Frank Lloyd Wright The Hollywood Pictures Backlot restroom is a combination of the Storer Residence and also **Freeman House** Year built: 1923 Architect: Frank Lloyd Wright	8161 Hollywood Blvd. 1962 Glencoe Way
PlayHouse Disney— Live on Stage	**ABC Radio Building** Formerly the Vitagraph Studios Year built: 1911 Architect: Auguste Bahrmann	4151 Prospect Ave.

APPENDIX E

A QUICK SYNOPSIS OF THE STORIES FROM THE PAINTINGS IN STORYTELLER'S CAFÉ

The original concept for Storyteller's Café was for the wait staff to tell you a story during your meal. Depending on the painting that you could see best, your waiter would weave the story throughout your meal. The restaurant soon realized that this took too much time away from delivering good food service so the idea was abolished. The décor, however, still remains. All the stories take place in California and give you a feeling of the history of the Golden State.

 LESSON TO LEARN

Although the name of the painter or painters has already been lost, the stories told in the artwork are some classic stories related to California. The authors are noteworthy, and although a short synopsis is described here, reading the original books is time well spent. In order from left to right the painters are:

The Cruise of 'the Dazzler' (1902) by Jack London

The novel *The Cruise of 'The Dazzler'* is a sailing adventure and a coming-of-age story set in San Francisco Bay. 'The Dazzler" is a ship and fifteen-year old Joe Bronson struggles with school, bullies, and girls, but dreams of running away to be a seaman, only to find that once he does run away and become a seaman, he longs to be home again. In the adventure, he discovers his moral ethics, a need for schooling, and meets a young friend nicknamed 'Frisco Kid. 'Frisco Kid never had the luxury of family, home, school, or even the acquaintance of girls. In the painting you'll see Joe in the striped shirt reading a map and 'Frisco Kid' is wearing sea-boots "which reach his hips." French Pete, the third man in the painting is the Captain of the Dazzler and forces the young boys into piracy. 'Frisco Kid is pointing to a map and a plan for escape.

The Mark of Zorro (1919) by Johnston McCulley

This was first released in 1919 as a five-part series titled *The Curse of Capistrano* in a pulp magazine *All-Story Weekly*. It was Douglas Fairbanks who read the pulp fiction and decided to make a movie. The film was re-titled *The Mark of Zorro* and it made Fairbanks' career and the character of Zorro legendary. The book was published in hardback for the first time in 1924 as *The Mark of Zorro*.

The story takes place in California around 1820. Don Diego Vega is an aristocrat who has a decadent life and no sense of responsibility. Don Diego's reputation is only a cover for his secret life as the masked hero Zorro. Zorro rides at the dark of night to correct the injustices of the times. He uses his sword to strike down those who exploit the poor and oppressed. The story has suspense, romance, and justice and is a wonderful read. In the Storyteller's painting of Zorro you see the wonderful rescue scene of Senorita Lolita, his true love. We know it's Zorro because the of black mask, black clothes, but most especially the "Z" on the breast plate of the horse. The scene actually takes place at night, but it would be hard to see the soldiers chasing and the plaza in the background from where Lolita is rescued.

LESSON TO LEARN

The story is set at the Mission San Juan Capistrano which is only 28 miles south of the Disneyland Resort. Well worth an afternoon, this is the legendary mission where the swallows return to visit around the 19th of March. The mission was established in 1776 by Friar Junipero Serra and known as the "Jewel" of the missions. The structure is believed to be the oldest church still standing in California.

Tortilla Flat by John Steinbeck
The story of Tortilla Flat was first published in 1935 and published in volumes *Steinbeck; Novels and Stories 1932-1937*. Tortilla Flat is a shabby hillside in Monterey California where the main character Danny inherits two houses. He and his friends known as paisanos, men of mixed heritage, settle there. One by one you learn of each man's character through adventures and mishaps. Without working or using money, this band of men typically find ways to acquire wine. The stories all come together in the end as Danny pursues the ultimate adventure.

In the Storyteller's café painting, "Pirate" or "Big Joe Portagee" is telling his five canine companions of his great honor in church. In a heart-warming thread among the chapters of Tortilla Flat, we learn that "Pirate" chops wood for a quarter a day. When one of his dogs was sick, he made a deal with God that if God spared the dog, Pirate would give the church a fine gold candelabra. After many years of chopping wood and not spending any money, the other characters realize that Pirate must have a large stash of money hidden in the forest. They try to con Pirate into giving them the money, but come to understand the treasure's higher purpose. Instead, the other characters decide to help Pirate save and prepare him for his honor in church, loaning him clothes so that he would be presentable. Ironically, none of Pirate's friends could see the preacher's sermon about Pirate because they lacked key pieces of clothing and the dogs simply weren't allowed in church. Pirate shares the moment privately in the woods with his closest friends.

The Californians (1898) by Gertrude Atherton
The story is about two girlfriends coming of age while living in San Francisco society in the era between Spanish rule and the American civilization. Magdelana, the

key character in the story, is rather plain, has difficulty expressing herself and is controlled by a dominant Spanish-American father. Her best friend and neighbor, Helena, is quite beautiful, out-spoken, and uncontrolled. The story is part romance, and part tragedy. When Helena throws a party while summering in Menlo Park, she meets an intriguing man and innocently falls in love with him, only to learn that he is Magdalena's fiancé. In the painting in Storyteller's Café, Magdalena is the dark-haired woman sitting facing her mother. The woman wearing the hat is a friend making a social call. At this point in the story, Helena is traveling to Europe and Magdalena is forced to stay home and listen again to the stories of the "old days" and the Spanish cotillions.

TREASURE & TRIVIA

Gertrude Atherton lived from 1857–1948 and was an early American feminist. She was one of a few women who earned a living as a writer and lived on the west coast. While visiting England, she made a special trip back to California to vote in the 1912 election where women had the first chance to participate in the vote. She developed her characters to represent California women as independent, morally upright, and able to speak their minds. The city of Atherton, Calif., was named for her husband's family and is about 386 miles north of the Disneyland Resort.

"Ahwahnee Tale" a Miwok Indian Legend

This portrait is of the Miwok Indians that live near Yosemite. Ahwahnee is the name of the tribe and the lodge. Although most of the murals in Storyteller's Café are depicting a specific story, this painting may not be specific to one particular story but to the general folklore of California's native people. If you'd like to read some of the legends, there is a fairly comprehensive book, "American Indian Myths and Legends" by Richard Erdoes and Alfonso Ortiz featuring 166 stories. Unlike Greek or Roman myths, the Native American stories are more organic originating from plants and animals. The beautiful painting in Storyteller's Café shows men sitting around a camp fire sharing a story about a bear. It's fun to think they're telling the story of Grizzly River Run.

The Celebrated Jumping Frog of Calaveras County (1864) by Mark Twain

This tall tale is a told with a series of unbelievable events, outrageous descriptions and is part of the Southwestern folklore. A chronic gambler, Jim Smiley trains his frog "Dan'l" to be an expert jumper and win him money in frog jumping contests. An out-of-towner meets Smiley and says he'd agree to take the bet except he doesn't have a frog. Since Smiley will do anything for a bet, he foolishly goes to the pond to get the stranger a frog, and asks him to watch his prize-winning frog, Dan'l. When Smiley isn't looking, the stranger dumps quail shot into Dan'l and you can guess the results of the contest. Some things worth noting in the painting, Jim Smiley is the man in the red vest. Notice how his frog appears to "weigh five pounds." The stranger has his hand in his pocket as if to hide something. The red building in the background says Calaveras to clue us into the story name and location. Smiley has had a mare in the story that the boys called "fifteen-minute nag" which you can also see in the painting. Smiley was always betting on the mare too, but it always had "asthma, or the distemper, or the consumption, or something of that kind."

Island of the Blue Dolphins by Scott O'Dell

Island of the Blue Dolphins is a story of a female Robinson Crusoe. Written in 1960, it won the John N. Newberry Medal for the Most Distinguished Contribution to American Literature for Children. The book is inspired by a true story of a woman who lived alone from 1835 to 1853 on what is now known as the Island of San Nicholas, some 75 miles southwest of Los Angeles. Her story became the legend of The Lost Woman of San Nicholas and she is buried on a hill near the Mission at Santa Barbara. The story crafted by Scott O'Dell uses what few facts that are known about her such as her jumping into the sea despite efforts to stop her. For 18 years she lived alone and her younger brother was killed by wild dogs, shortly after she was left on the island. It is also known that she tamed a dog for companionship and she made a skirt of green cormorant feathers. The feather skirt still hangs in a museum in Rome. The book weaves stories of her finding food, building a shelter, making weapons, fighting her enemies, battling loneliness, and attempting to leave the island. In the story her name is Won-a-pa-lei, which means Girl with Long Black Hair, although she has a secret name: Karana. She sometimes made a wreath of flowers for her and her dog Rontu and would walk around the island. She always carried the spears around the island to protect herself from the wild dogs. Another enemy is an Aleut ship that came to hunt sea otter. The first time the Aleut ship visited the island, there was a terrible battle where most of the tribe and her family were killed. It was for the remaining tribe's safety that the people soon left the island. When Karana realized her brother was left alone on the island, she jumped overboard to stay with her younger brother until another ship came for them. This painting depicts a later scene in the novel and allows you to wonder if the ship in the background is the Aleut ship returning for the hunt or another ship for her rescue.

 LESSON TO LEARN

The book refers to an Aleut ship. The Aleutian Islands are the far western islands of Alaska, spreading to Russia.

BIBLIOGRAPHY

1. *Jim Henson: The Works; The Art, the Magic, the Imagination* by Christopher Finch, 1993, pages 40, 146-154, 220-227.
2. "California Dreamin'" by Lorraine Santoli, Disney Magazine, Spring 2001, pages 36-40.
3. "Thank you Cast" by Chela Castano-Lenahan, The Disneyland Resort Line, Vol. 33, number 6, page 4.
4. "Special Olympian and Family Become First Guests" by Chela Castāno-Lenhan, Vol. 33, number 7, page 3.
5. "Die-Hard Fans Waited it Out" by Chela Castāno -Lenhan, Vol. 33, number 7, page 3.
6. "Surrounded by Stars on the Red Carpet" by Chela Castāno-Lenhan, Vol. 33, number 7, page 3.
7. Disneyland Resort Grand Opening Festivities, February 8, 2001, cast member video.
8. "California Adventure" by Alexandra Kennedy, Disney Magazine, Spring 2001, pages 32-35.
9. "Golden State" by Kevin Markey, Disney Magazine, Spring 2001, pages 42-48.
10. "Hollywood Pictures Backlot" by Kevin Markey, Disney Magazine, Spring 2001, pages 50-54.
11. "Paradise Pier" by Kevin Markey, Disney Magazine, Spring 2001, pages 56-61.
12. "Ten Reasons to Stay at Disney's Grand Californian" by Lisa Oppenheimer, Disney Magazine, Spring 2001, pages 68-69.
13. "Downtown Disney" by Kevin Markey, Disney Magazine, Spring 2001, pages 70-71.
14. "Disney A to Z: The Updated Official Encyclopedia" by Dave Smith, pages 13, 14, 42, 148, 203, 204, 205, 267, 280, 292, 388, 566, 576.
15. "Backstage – Moonlighting Monsters," By Lisa Oppenheimer, Disney Magazine, Fall 2001, page 73.
16. "The Disney Traveler Parks and Beyond: What's New, What's Great, What's a Deal," by Liz Smith, Disney Magazine, Fall 2001, page 17.
17. "Backstage Pass Our Roving Photographers Take You There – Soundstage Dedication" by Alexandra Kennedy, Disney Magazine, Winter 2001-2002, page 29.
18. "The Secrets of Monsters, Inc. Hidden details, inside jokes, and (how-they-did-that's.)" by Leonard Maltin, Disney Magazine, Winter 2001-2002, pages 30-35.
19. *Walt's Revolution!: By the Numbers,* by Harrison "Buzz" Price, Ripley Entertainment Inc. 2003 pages 26-37.
20. "Greene & Greene" by Edward R. Bosley, Phaidon Press, pages 40-70.
21. "Disney's Arts & Crafts Showpiece" American Bungalow, by Michelle Gringeri-Brown, pages 48-62
22. Frank Lloyd Wright Preservation Trust catalog.
23. *Around the World with Disney* by Kevin Markey, Disney Editions, New York, 2005, pages 18, 34, 36, 66, 73, 83, 90, 101, 110, 114, 115,

122, 125, 127, 136, 162, 167, 168, 172.
24. *www.Pixar.com website*
25. *movies.yahoo.com website*
26. *www.ibdb.com website*
    a. Jerry Orbach
    b. David Ogden Stiers
    c. The Little Shop of Horrors,
    d. The Glass Menagerie
    e. My Fair Lady
    f. Annie
    g. Beauty and the Beast
    h. A Chorus Line
    i. West Side Story
    j. Barefoot in the Park
    k. A Streetcar Named Desire
    l. The King and I
    m. John Steinbeck
27. *us.imdb.com website*
    a. Finding Nemo
    b. Muppet Vision 3-D
    c. Ben-Hur
    d. The Seven Year Itch
    e. Gone with the Wind
    f. Monsters Inc.
    g. John Lasseter
    h. John Ratzenberger
    i. Denis Leary
    j. Jim Henson
    k. David Ogden Stiers
    l. Jerry Orbach
    m. Pancho Barnes
    n. Adrian Adolph Greenburg
    o. William Shatner
    p. Burgess Meredith
    q. Tower of Terror
28. *www.usc.edu/isd/archives/la/scandals/st_francis_dam.html* for St. Francis Dam information
29. *www.ennishouse.org* for Frank Lloyd Wright Los Angeles homes
30. *www.uh.edu/engines/epi1278.htm* for Quonset Hut Engines by John H. Lienhard
31. *http://you-are-here.com/building* Los Angeles Architectural Photo Gallery

a. Argyle Hotel
b. Bullock's Wilshire
c. Chapman Market
d. Los Angeles Theater
e. Wiltern Theater
f. El Capitan Theater
g. Farmer's Market
h. Lloyd Wright Home Studio
i. Max Factor Make-up Studio
j. Pantages Theater Hollywood
32. "The Lay of the Land" by Lee Macdonald *Tales from the Laughing Place,* issue 3, July 2005, pages 13-15.
33. *www.edwards.af.mil*
    a. Charles "Chuck" Yeager
34. *www.RussianRiverTravel.com*
35. *www.centennialofflight.gov*
    a. Jacqueline "Jackie" Cochran
    b. Donald Douglas
    c. Chuck Yeager
    d. Howard Hughes
    e. James H. Doolittle
    f. Lockheed Martin Corporation
    g. Glenn L. Martin
    h. Amelia Earhart
    i. Florence Lowe "Pancho" Barnes
36. *www.newscientist.com* "First speed of gravity measurement revealed" by Hazel Muir, January 7, 2003
37. *www.earlyaviators.com*
    a. Alys McKey Bryant
38. *www.flyingmachines.org*
    a. John Montgomery
39. *www.sandiegohistory.org*
    a. John J. Montgomery bio
40. Pioneers of Flight home page, *www.nasm.si.edu*
    a. Gossamer Condor
    b. Lockheed 5B Vega
41. *en.wikipedia.org*
    a. Speed of Light
    b. Gossamer Condor
    c. John J. Montgomery

   d. Donald Douglas
   e. Pelton Wheel
   f. Charles Yeager
   g. Howard Hughes
   h. John K. Northrop
   i. Jimmy D oolittle
   j. Glenn L. Martin Company
   k. James Herman Banning
   l. Alys McKey Bryant
   m. César Chávez
   n. Steve Jobs
   o. Steven Wozniak
   p. Robert Mondavi
   q. Dorothea Lang
   r. John Muir
   s. John Steinbeck

42. *www.asiansinamerica.org*
   a. Katherine Cheung

43. *www.awam.org/Katherine Cheung.htm*
   a. Katherine Cheung

44. *www.scifi.com/twilightzone/*
   a. The After Hours
   b. Time Enough at Last
   c. A Stop at Willoughby
   d. A Passage for Trumpet
   e. Long Distance Call
   f. A Thing About Machines
   g. A Most Unusual Camera
   h. Twenty-two
   i. The Invaders
   j. To Serve Man
   k. Little Girl Lost
   l. A Kind of Stopwatch
   m. Nick of Time
   n. It's a Good Life
   o. Kick the Can
   p. A World of His Own

45. *www.allstar.fiu.edu*
   a. Glenn L. Martin
   b. Donald W. Douglas
   c. Charles E. "Chuck" Yeager
   d. Howard Hughes
   e. John K. Northrop
   f. Jacqueline "Jackie" Cochran

46. *G is for Golden: A California Alphabet,* by David Domeniconi, Sleeping Bear Press, 2005

47. *www.hiddenmickey.org*
   a. Disney's California Adventure; Sunshine Plaza
   b. Disney's California Adventure; Golden State, Grizzly Peak Recreation Area
   c. Disney's California Adventure; Hollywood Pictures Backlot
   d. Disney's California Adventure; Paradise Pier

48. *Disney the First 100 Years:* by Dave Smith and Steven B. Clark, published by Hyperion, 1999, page 194.

49. *www.laughingplace.com/Info-ID-DL-Windows.asp,* Disneyland Windows on Main Street, July 30, 2000

50. Communications from Dave Smith at Walt Disney Archives

UPDATES

In October of 2007, the Walt Disney Company announced a major expansion to Disney's California Adventure. Disney President and Chief Executive Officer Bob Iger and Parks & Resorts Chairman Jay Rasulo announced the expansion is an investment of $1.1 billion. The project is a multi-year plan adding major attractions throughout the park.

This announcement was preceded by another significant milestone in June of 2006 when Bob Iger solidified the merger with Pixar for $7.4 billion. In doing so Imagineers now had many additional characters to develop attractions around. *Disney's California Adventure Detective* has quickly become an historical perspective of the opening years of DCA. To keep current of the amazing transformation and stay abreast of all the Hidden Mickeys and fun trivia, log onto www.themeparkdetective.com for free updates.

Paradise Pier will get an extreme makeover with the additions of *Toy Story Midway Mani*a!, a Little Mermaid attraction, and a unique nighttime water spectacular with new seating and viewing for 9,000 guests.

A new area called *Cars Land* will add 12 acres to the Disney's California Adventure Park. Inspired by the 2006 Pixar film *Cars,* guests will jump into Radiator Springs Racers for an "E-Ticket" experience. After a briefing from Lightning McQueen and Doc, guests will race around hairpin turns and steep banks immersing themselves in the middle of the *Cars* world.

Photos by Russell Trahan

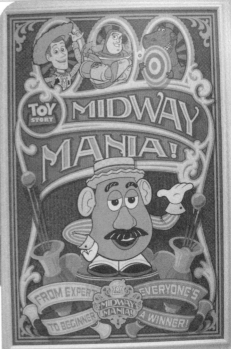

The entry plaza and gateway will all see an extreme makeover as the new entrance will be reminiscent of the California that Walt Disney experienced when he came to Southern California in the 1920s. The Los Angeles movie palace, Carthay Circle Theater, inspired the new icon for the park entrance. This historic theater has significance as the premier of *Snow White and the Seven Dwarfs*, the first full-length animated film debuted there in 1937. The DCA Carthay Circle-like Theater is expected to house Walt Disney's personal story of coming to California. Locals who remember the Red Car Trolleys of the old Pacific Electric Railway may be happy to see the return of the public transportation system. The new DCA Red Car Trolleys will travel guests up and down the new Main Street.

Again for free updates log onto www.themeparkdetective.com for current attractions and trivia!

INDEX

ABOUT THE AUTHOR

Kendra Trahan was born and educated in southern Oregon. Although she grew up only 21 miles away from California's northern border, she longed to be the kind of "California girl" that the Beach Boys were inspired to sing about.

Lucky to live in Southern California when Disney's California Adventure opened, she jumped at the chance when the Walt Disney Company announced their pre-opening days. Although it was one of the coolest winters for Southern California, she was one of the first to ride Grizzly River Run, learning that wet jeans never seem to dry.

Disneyland continues to be her favorite Park of all the Disney Parks, but Disney's California Adventure is a nice place to relax, and enjoy a glass of wine. There are a few highlights such as *Screamin, Soarin'*, and the *Animation building* that keep her coming back. After spending six years of research, she has a greater appreciation for Disney's California Adventure.

Kendra realized that the Imagineers have done their homework and she found that the Park is rich with details and tributes. Although Disney's California Adventure has seen a lot of changes, Kendra eagerly awaits the renovation planned that is as significant as the 1959 renovation to Tomorrowland at Disneyland.

Kendra serves as National President of the National Fantasy Fan Club (NFFC), the club for Disney enthusiasts. She is a member of the board of governors of Carolwood Pacific Historical Society, and also the board of directors for Walt Disney's barn museum in Los Angeles' Griffith Park. After the success of her first book *Disneyland Detective*, Kendra decided to pursue writing the series and share trivia about Disney's California Adventure. Shortly after writing the book, she moved to Orlando, Fla., with her husband to continue research on the Walt Disney World resort and cruise line.

Any given weekend you may see her enjoying Walt Disney World with her husband or asking friends to help plan the next big NFFC convention. Introduce yourself as a Disneyland Detective and share your favorite Disney experience. As the song says in *Just One Dream* from the Disney's California Adventure attraction *Golden Dreams*, "like the promise of sun, we're born to shine."

Karl Yamauchi is a native Californian and was excited to participate in *Disney's California Adventure Detective* because his task was related to his favorite attraction in the Park. You'll find his artistic talent in the *Soarin'* appendix as he illustrated the airplanes found in the queue. He claims that "*Soarin' Over California*, is the best family ride that Disney has ever done."

Karl's Christmas cards are treasured gifts by his friends. He is a retired bridge architect by profession, and a fervent Disney Fan by choice. Karl and his wife Nancy are members of Carolwood Pacific Historical Society and important members of the Florida Planning Committee for the National Fantasy Fan Club. They live in Celebration, Fla., and enjoy running Disney marathons, playing golf, and working part-time at the Walt Disney World Resort.

After a successful venture with *Disneyland Detective*, I was happy to join forces with **Debbie Smith** again for *Disney's California Adventure Detective*. Luckily she had taken photos of DCA while the Park was still under construction, renting hotel rooms from nearby hotels to get different vantage points. As a native Californian, exploring the Park with her was fun and exciting as she could point nuances to me that only the natives pick up. One particular assignment was quite entertaining as she entered Grizzly River Run to photograph the hieroglyphics on the inside of the mountain. Although she loaded thousands of dollars worth of camera equipment onto the raft, everyone else seemed panicked. Debbie being the consummate professional, endured splash, and dizziness and risked it all to capture the necessary shots. Debbie has a portfolio of dramatic landscape photographs specializing in Yosemite, the ghost town and Bodie State Park. Both Debbie and her husband Martin are members of the Carolwood Pacific Historical Society.

It was an honor to partner again with **Brian McKim** for the portrait illustrations, this time for *Disney's California Adventure Detective*. Brian was born and raised in Southern California, a child of a Disney employee. Brian is the eldest son of Disney Legend Sam McKim, who spent 32 years at Walt Disney Imagineering. Since the publication of *Disneyland Detective*, Sam McKim has been honored with a window on Main Street U.S.A. in Disneyland.

This time *Disney's California Adventure Detective* highlighted people who Brian didn't necessarily know, but are famous people who helped create California history. One of his favorite illustrations was of John Lasseter, since he and John are friends. Designing his shirt for the portrait was particularly fun in highlighting John's favorite Pixar characters. Brian's favorite attraction in DCA is the Animation Building in Hollywood Pictures Backlot.

Brian earned his Bachelor of Arts from California State University at Northridge, and B.F.A. from the Art Center College of Design in Pasadena. Brian then went to work at Walt Disney Studios for 15 years in feature animation. He especially likes painting landscapes and portraitures in oils. For relaxation he likes to spend time with his wife Dorothy, son Tyler, and daughter Natalie. Whenever Brian has some free time, he likes to take the family fishing.

ORDER FORM

If this is a library copy, please photocopy this page.

Ship Books to:

Name:_____

Address:_____

City:_____State:_____Zip:_____

Quantity   _____ Disneyland Detective (soft cover $19.95)

_____ Disney's California Adventure Detective ($14.95)

$_____ Postage add $2 for first book

$_____ Add $1 each additional book

$_____ Sales Tax:
California Residents only, please add 7.75%

$_____ **Amount Enclosed**

Checks, Money orders, Major credit cards Visa accepted.

Credit Card #_____

Exp. Date _____ / _____

Name on Card_____

PermaGrin
PUBLISHING, INC.
27758 Santa Margarita Parkway #379
Mission Viejo, CA 92691